MORE
SCENES AND
MONOLOGS
from the best
NEW PLAYS

An anthology of new
dramatic writing
from professionally
produced plays

edited by

ROGER ELLIS

MERIWETHER PUBLISHING LTD.
Colorado Springs, Colorado

Meriwether Publishing Ltd., Publisher
PO Box 7710
Colorado Springs, CO 80933-7710

Executive editor: Theodore O. Zapel
Cover design: Jan Melvin

Library of Congress Cataloging-in-Publication Data

More scenes and monologs from the best new plays : an anthology of new dramatic writing from professionally produced plays / edited by Roger Ellis.
    p. cm.
ISBN 13: 978-1-56608-142-9 (pbk.)
ISBN 10: 1-56608-142-4 (pbk.)
1. Acting. 2. Monologues. 3. American drama—20th century.
I. Ellis, Roger, 1943 May 18-
  PN2080.M675 2007
  812'.04508—dc22

                    2006035093

1   2   3   07   08   09

Contents

Monologs for Women 135

Monologs for Men 175

Editor's Introduction

How to use the Collection

This text presents a range of monologs and scenes for students in their mid-teens to mid-twenties, drawn from contemporary plays recently produced in North America and Europe. It also contains a tip sheet for preparing and rehearsing the material, nineteen useful exercises for strengthening oral presentation and acting skills, and a list of resources for further investigation. The book is intended as a text for work and study by individuals or groups in class and studio settings.

One noteworthy feature of this anthology is the fact that I've purposely selected its contents from unpublished plays, except in a handful of cases. This means that you won't be able to refer to the context of the entire script in order to interpret the behavior of the characters or the dramatic action of the scenes. Instead, the collection compels you to exercise your imaginative skills in a heightened way by making original and often personal choices for assigning motivations, discovering physical actions, establishing relationships, and so forth. Readers seeking the full text of a play can sometimes refer to the playwrights' credits section where play publishers, when available, are listed under the title.

Also noteworthy is the widely different length of the extracts included here. My intention was to include pieces as short as sixty seconds or as long as seven to eight minutes within a single volume so that the collection could help you learn many fundamental acting skills besides auditioning. I've discovered, for example, that acting students who wish to concentrate solely upon shorter pieces (which are often required in competitive audition contexts), can profit immensely from editing down a longer piece. Editing down teaches you to cut to the chase, sharpening your skills with storytelling, playing events, and developing effective contrasts and conflicts in short, compressed extracts. On the other hand, if you prefer to create more complex characters and multifaceted relationships, you can avail yourself of the longer extracts. In fact, several of the selections are complete one-act plays that can be performed in less than ten minutes (*Rockettes, Falling, Jennie*, and some others).

The supplementary material that follows the monologs and scenes (tip sheet, exercises, useful books) appears in response to a large number of teachers who have asked for suggestions when

1

directing rehearsals or working the material in class settings. Most of the exercises are taken from my auditioning textbook, *The Complete Audition Book for Young Actors* (Meriwether, 2003). These have been developed over years of teaching university actors in scene, monolog, and auditioning classes; and from numerous workshops for professionals and amateurs that I've conducted in the Americas and Europe. I've found that these basic exercises produce excellent results with students of high school age and above; while the list of selected resources includes those books and Web sites that my own college-level students regard as the most useful and relevant to their work.

Selection Criteria

I've selected the extracts in this anthology according to several well-defined criteria. First, all the work included here is taken from plays that have enjoyed a production in some form: staged readings, in-progress workshops, or fully-staged shows. This requirement is the best litmus test of a play's quality because only in the crucible of public performance can the strengths and weaknesses of a new work be detected. Only a live audience will tell a writer many things about how his or her play can relate to and communicate with spectators moment-by-moment, as good writing for the stage must always do. You can be confident that all the selections here are strongly playable and written expressly to be spoken and presented.

I've also paid special attention to the gender balance of the entire collection when deciding which plays to include and which not. Thus, there are more selections for women here than for men, a fact that seems to me to reflect the gender makeup of most acting classes and workshops I've taught at various age levels. But there are also unisex pieces here in which the characters are gender-neutral. Ry Herman's *Voices in My Head*, Ruben Carbajal's *Portland*, or Mark Wheeller's *Missing Dan Nolan* are examples of extracts that can be interestingly explored by reversing the gender of the characters. And there may also be more, depending upon your approach to the scene or monolog.

I've avoided including any classical material in the collection and chosen only contemporary work written within the past decade. I've done this in part because classical material, while extremely challenging, is already well represented in specialized anthologies, while this collection is geared to cutting-edge work that is less well known and available. Additionally, classical material requires unique and special skills that many young actors simply haven't developed. Finally, I think that young students in general find recent topics, language, and stage conventions more relevant and accessible to them, and therefore you'll be able to show yourself in a better, more confident light. Contemporaneity often invites a closer identification with the dramatic relationships and situations than older plays can accomplish and carries the added benefit of avoiding shopworn characters and conventions of social manners and language that may seem artificial to you.

I've been very careful, of course, to select material that is age-appropriate for students from their mid-teens to mid-twenties. I feel strongly that every actor, regardless of age, should always try to play to his or her strengths when presenting a monolog or scene. There are certainly occasions when you'll need to "stretch" yourself with very challenging material, but I regularly advise my own students to avoid attempting this in competitive situations like trying-out for roles or winning scholarships or participating in contests. Finding material that is appropriate for you means finding monologs and scenes within your emotional range, a range that will gradually expand and deepen as you gain more experience.

Language and Characters in the Collection

While guided by the criteria just mentioned, I've especially tried to create a body of work here that presents a broad spectrum of language challenges for you. Teachers struggle relentlessly with this, training you to appreciate the flexibility, power, subtlety, musicality, and expressiveness of words. Certainly our electronic age has done much to reduce language to the level of pure function and denotative meaning. Most of us are only rarely conscious of continually shaping our discourse for speaking effectively; we just talk and everyone accepts that that's honest communication. Interestingly enough, even in a society that is so dominated by hack writing for pop magazines, commercial advertisements, motion pictures, and TV shows, many Hollywood acting coaches have told me how rare and exciting it is to find a young actor who does know how to speak well, who understands how to enter into the thought processes of a human being through his or her language, and who possesses techniques for rendering that character convincingly and naturally through his or her language.

3

You should also realize that an actor is not primarily concerned with directly expressing himself or herself through art; he or she is instead an interpreter of others' words. While all of us, actors included, strive to be perceived as sincere in what we say, the actor's task is to make another person's words seem sincere — not his or her own. Thus, it's irrelevant to ask an actor doing a TV commercial whether or not he believes that a certain brand of dog food is good for his pet, or whether an actress portraying Ophelia believes that Ophelia is justified in surrendering to despair. The job of the actor is to do these things as though the character believed they were right to do. In our modern world, great emphasis is placed upon communication skills, which generally means self-expression: the ability to form ideas, to articulate them effectively and persuasively to others, to join in the public or corporate debates over issues and workaday problems. While many can do this with success — both in the workplace as well as in blog sites and other informal contexts — none of this self-expression has anything to do with what an actor must accomplish.

Some of the selections in this anthology, of course, will offer you dialog in an everyday realistic form which is the most accessible to you no matter what experience you've already had. Be careful, though, because while remaining conversational, writers often pattern such discourse in ways that require interpretation beyond that of natural conversation. In other words, you can't just start talking it. In good writing, for example, pauses are carefully and deliberately placed (*Voices in My Head*), short and choppy sentences are reflective of important thought processes (*Falling*), and clichés and slang can become key indicators of character traits (*By Looking*). This is why doing a paraphrase of your text (one of the exercises included at the end of this book) is a crucial first step since it will reveal how differently you think and speak and feel than the character does.

There are also a number of pieces whose language will challenge you with heightened lyricism that is not everyday or natural in any sense of the word. Speaking these lines realistically will seem very phony to you. You have to be emotionally and spiritually up for it. For example, the scene between Nancy and Sylvia taken from *Have Mercy* leads Nancy to the point of almost religious ecstasy when she breaks into those long passages expressing her guilt and fear of damnation. Similarly, Cody's reverie from *Harvest* about his boyhood is a nostalgic and poetic account of how good his life used to be — and can only be motivated by the sensitive young woman who is hanging on every word of his lyrical fantasy. You have to let yourself go with language like this: let yourself slide intuitively into the character's world and feel their emotional condition instead of simply reading words off the page and hoping their plain sense meaning will express the heartbeats of the character. Remember: this character is not you; he or she is different from you. And many of those differences will be reflected in his or her language.

Other selections will ask you to create a huge subtext with your words in order to reveal what the character is really saying. This is where modern plays differ so radically from classical pieces — there is no subtext in Shakespeare. When paraphrasing these modern selections, you must read between the lines that are only tips of a huge subsurface iceberg of emotions, past experiences, or tangled relationships. This is the way in which modern playwrights work. These characters rarely say what's on their minds. They dance around painful conflicts, embarrassing admissions, and paralyzing fears, and you can't simply rip the lines off and skate across the surface of the text. Cyndi's painful confession to Paul of her superficiality when she claims she really feels unworthy of his love in *The Gifted Program*, or Kendra's hilarious pretended innocence in *Shot At* as she questions Jason about the "mysterious" gunshot are good examples of how a rich subtext must inform your interpretation as you speak. And as you might expect, some subtexts are easy to spot while others will challenge you maddeningly!

And then, of course, there is the most challenging language of all: language that demands that you reveal yourself at your most vulnerable, where cardboard emotions or indicating will never convince an audience. Tristram's admission to his girlfriend of his boring, dull personality in *Suburban Redux* will make the listener squirm in his seat only if you can speak the monolog as honestly and simply and personally as possible, hiding nothing. Nor can you avoid or down-pedal the absolute intensity required by the character of Zinni in *Window of Opportunity* who must speak as though having a child were food and water and breath itself to her. Nothing less than passionate conviction and belief will work for you in performance of texts like these. They'll force you to touch bottom with all your emotional resources, using yourself to bring these characters to life.

In addition to the language challenges that you'll encounter in the book, you'll also find an excitingly unique gallery of characters to portray. Hopefully you'll enjoy discovering many of those roles within your own personality (because using yourself is what acting is really all about); but even when this isn't the case, you'll likely find yourself fascinated by the dreams and disillusionment, the brilliance and the charm, the loves and hates and fears of the characters who live within these pages.

Some of these roles are straightforward and familiar in the sense that you might very well encounter their emotions and needs in your ordinary everyday life. For example, the teen runaway Jennie, the title character of Meri Wallace's play, opens a touching window for us into that difficult moment of decision-making when she decides whether or not to leave her suburban life for something — anything — that might promise something better at this critical point. Similarly, Bernie and Evie in Faye Sholiton's *V-E Day* strike a familiar chord of young love as they meet and fall for each other during the heady and exhilarating days on the home front in World War II. Or Lulu and Dana in Shirley King's *Donny's Diner* might be any young professional women sitting across from you in a deli, gossiping about their careers and relationships and what they plan to do together that evening.

Other characters are not so ordinary, and in fact may even border on loony. There are the two brothers, for example, Hans and Johan, doing a twisted, comic, sibling rap-routine on a Christmas-theme in Lindsay Price's *Deck the Stage*. Similarly, you may find it incredible to imagine that a modern youngster like Baby, in Gwendolyn Schwinke's *Thrown by Angels*, could be so completely unaware of the society around her after being raised by a loopy dad who confined her in the house and raped her for years. And is young Tomlyn in Elise Geither's *The Doe*, suffering from a too-vivid imagination that borders on lunacy when her nightmare begins to intrude upon her waking moments?

Finally, there are other roles here in the collection that may ask you to stretch your imagination in order to discover life from a radically different standpoint than what you've been used to. Rebar and Soran, for example, young immigrants on-the-make from Kurdistan in Deborah Brevoort's *The Poetry of Pizza*, actually sit and weep copiously together in the kitchen over the lack of fresh pistachios (before "the girl" enters the restaurant). Him and Her in Matéi Visniec's *The Story of the Panda Bears* need you to express their love with passionate conviction and exhilaration sparked by their mutual obsession — a relationship that seems ultimately to break down by the end of the scene.

Try to avoid the impulse to skim through the selections here, and instead take the time to read each of them aloud, listening to the heartbeats of what these characters are expressing and sensing your own personal response to their words as you do so. Such moments of honesty, discovery, and self-realization present great opportunities for you to use yourself and compel the listeners' attention. Open your imagination to the urge you'll feel for inventing a history or personal circumstance to their lives — the character biography or backstory that motivates them. Zero-in on what possible reasons they may have for speaking to each other, and what they absolutely must communicate to us in the speech or the scene.

If you challenge yourself to pique the listeners' curiosity, to move them to sympathy, to share in your character's laughter or fear or sorrow or joy in the space of a minute or two, then you'll be doing yeoman's work as an actor. You'll compel others to watch, listen, and share in your experience as you tell these characters' stories in performance. The short acting prefaces before each selection will guide you towards the heart of the writing, and the class exercises at the end of the book will certainly sharpen your acting skills if you perform them religiously. The rest is up to you!

A Reminder about Cultural and Intellectual Property

In all the anthologies I edit, I feel compelled to remind readers that the work in the collection is intended *only* for studio exercises or for reading. When it comes to performing it, producing it in public readings, or adapting it in any way via the electronic media for other audiences — educational, amateur, or professional — then permission *must* be obtained and royalties paid to the agent or author.

Perhaps this caution needs to be frequently restated in this age of the Internet where so much is available online or otherwise reproducible at little or no charge. Readers must remind themselves that plays — like other unique, cultural artifacts — are not equivalent to the cheapened bytes and factoids we slug through and manipulate by the thousands every day. They are the intellectual property of human beings who have spent many years earning, and who therefore deserve, proper acknowledgment and compensation for producing and distributing them to the public.

Bear in mind that I'm attempting in this book to highlight and promote the work of a handful of uniquely talented and very highly motivated artists whose worth, importance, and cultural value in our society is already deeply discounted, frequently debased, and even despised. Their plays are their honest work — their products. Pay for them. If you wish to perform any of these monologs in public, credits appear at the end of this volume; call or write for permission. These artists are not unreasonable in what they expect from us.

Scenes for Two Women

Rockettes
by Jonathan Wallace

Bree – 21   **Seriocomic**
Bryony – 21

Bree and Bryony are close friends, but in this encounter they make discoveries about each other and themselves that drive the two apart at the scene's conclusion. Structurally, the scene is built around one character who is role-playing and concealing, while the other experiences a series of discoveries as she gradually learns the truth. Each is profoundly different at the end than she was at the beginning. In addition to the clearly constructed story line, the actresses should pay attention to the contrast between the two women: Bryony, who is naïve and wide-eyed yet very smart, and Bree, who seems very cynical and tough but who also has a vulnerable side that she tries to hide. As the scene begins, the women have just gotten off the bus in Manhattan, and Bryony is asleep on a park bench. Bree is placing some belongings, including a CD player, into a large floppy canvas handbag. She looks at Bryony, starts to leave, then comes back and shakes her awake.

1   **BRYONY: Omigod, Bree, are we being arrested?**
2   **BREE: No, you were sleeping.**
3   **BRYONY: I was dreaming we robbed a bank.** *(BRYONY takes a*
4   *notebook from her own large floppy bag and begins to*
5   *write.)*
6   **BREE: I have to talk to you.**
7   **BRYONY: Wait, I have to write this down.**
8   **BREE: Do it later.**
9   **BRYONY: I always write my dreams down while they're fresh in**
10   **my mind.** *(BREE makes a face; BRYONY scribbles.)* **That's**
11   **good. What did you want to talk about?**
12 **BREE:** *(Looks at notebook; reads.)* **"We were robbing a bank."**
13   **You didn't think you would remember that later?**

1   BRYONY: You *never* remember your dreams.

2   BREE: We need to change our plans.

3   BRYONY: We just got here.

4   BREE: It's not gonna work out.

5   BRYONY: What?

6   BREE: You should go back to San Jose.

7   BRYONY: *(Shocked)* Why?

8   BREE: *(At a loss)* I'm trying to get stuff done and you're

9   sleeping.

10 BRYONY: I didn't feel well.

11 BREE: When I needed to get organized at the Port Authority,

12   you were gone almost a half hour.

13 BRYONY: I was throwing up in the bathroom.

14 BREE: I told you I couldn't baby sit you in New York.

15 BRYONY: I feel better now. Did you call your friends yet?

16 BREE: No, I couldn't leave you alone on this bench.

17 BRYONY: *(Looking around, a bit alarmed)* Why? Brooklyn

18   doesn't look dangerous.

19 BREE: Every place is dangerous. It's gonna be a much harder

20   job than I thought, looking after you.

21 BRYONY: I never asked you to look after me.

22 BREE: You're too soft to be here.

23 BRYONY: What are you saying?

24 BREE: I think you should go back.

25 BRYONY: I just need a good night's rest. Those burritos we

26   brought on the bus killed my stomach.

27 BREE: There's no place for you to get a night's rest. I couldn't

28   find my friend.

29 BRYONY: I thought you didn't call her.

30 BREE: Well, I did, from the Port Authority, while you were

31   puking. Her number is disconnected. We have no place to

32   stay.

33 BRYONY: Omigod. Why didn't you tell me?

34 BREE: I just did.

35 BRYONY: Don't you have other friends here?

1 BREE: No.

2 BRYONY: You said you knew like a million people.

3 BREE: Well, I don't.

4 BRYONY: We have to find a hotel.

5 BREE: We can't afford a hotel in New York, they're like a
6   thousand dollars a night.

7 BRYONY: So now you want to go back?

8 BREE: I'm gonna stay, even if I have to sleep on the street.
9   You're gonna go back.

10 BRYONY: We're going to audition for the Rockettes.

11 BREE: *(Impatient)* No, we're not. You can't have a tattoo and be
12   a Rockette.

13 BRYONY: Who says?

14 BREE: It's right on the Web site, which you never even read.

15   *(They look at each other. BRYONY is shocked as she*
16   *processes this information; BREE is realizing she has made*
17   *a tactical error.)*

18 BRYONY: *(Brow furrowed)* You knew that before we started?

19 BREE: No, I just found out.

20 BRYONY: Bullshit, you looked at it weeks ago.

21 BREE: I didn't want to tell you; you'd be too upset.

22 BRYONY: You *made* me get this tattoo. *(Thinks.)* You didn't want
23   me to be a Rockette?

24 BREE: *(Blowing up)* Who the hell wants to be a Rockette? You're
25   so lame.

26 BRYONY: Why did you ask me to come to New York?

27 BREE: *(She has decided that brutal honesty is the best way to get*
28   *rid of BRYONY.)* I was supposed to go with Charisma but
29   she got born again.

30 BRYONY: You don't want to dance?

31 BREE: I am gonna dance.

32 BRYONY: Omigod ... without me?

33 BREE: I met a guy who says he's gonna get me a job at Scores.

34 BRYONY: You're going to *strip*?

35 BREE: Whatever it takes. I'm not going home ever. *(Pause.)* You

1   should leave.

2   BRYONY: When did you meet him?

3   BREE: While you were in the bathroom.

4   BRYONY: Omigod, was it that guy?

5   BREE: Yeah.

6   BRYONY: You told me that was some creep coming on to you.

7   BREE: He was, but he said he could get me a job.

8   BRYONY: Did it occur to you he might be lying?

9   BREE: He had a card.

10 BRYONY: *(Persuasive as possible)* Bree, let's put our thinking

11   caps on, we'll come up with something.

12 BREE: *(Childish imitation)* "Let's put our thinking caps on."

13   *(Angry)* I don't need to come up with something. I can

14   make mad money at Scores. *(They stare at each other.)*

15 BRYONY: Nasty girls work at Scores.

16 BREE: *(Indignant)* I'm not nasty.

17 BRYONY: You will be if you work there.

18 BREE: You're a lousy dancer.

19 BRYONY: Don't leave me here.

20 BREE: I'm gonna meet the guy at eleven and I want you gone by

21   then.

22 BRYONY: Did you take my ring?

23 BREE: What the hell are you talking about?

24 BRYONY: I saw you take it on the bus. I thought it was a dream

25   because Brad Pitt was there. *(Pages through her notebook.)*

26   See: "Bree and Brad Pitt stole my ring." *(BREE slaps the*

27   *notebook out of her hands. BRYONY grabs BREE's*

28   *pocketbook and they fight over it. BRYONY succeeds in*

29   *dumping the contents of BREE's bag on to the bench and the*

30   *pavement and spots the ring, which she puts on her finger.*

31   *BREE starts picking everything up and putting it back in her*

32   *bag.)*

33 BREE: *(Vicious)* Will you please go now?

34 BRYONY: I will if you'll do our routine one last time.

35 BREE: What?!

1   **BRYONY: You heard me. Do our dance one more time and I'll**
2   **go.**
3   **BREE: You're crazy.**
4   **BRYONY: If you don't, I'm going to tell your stepfather where**
5   **you are.**
6   **BREE: You would do that?**
7   **BRYONY: Yes.**
8   **BREE: That damned psycho would come to New York and pull**
9   **me out of Scores, you know that?**
10 **BRYONY: I hope he does.**
11 **BREE: He had sex with me.**
12 **BRYONY: I don't believe you.**
13 **BREE: It's true.** *(They glare at each other.)* **If I do that stupid**
14   **dance you'll screw-off and leave me alone?**
15 **BRYONY: Yes.**
16 **BREE: All right.** *(BREE starts the CD player and they do an inept*
17   *but rather charming attempt at a Rockette routine together.)*
18 **BREE: You happy now?**
19 **BRYONY: We are so great together, Bree.**
20 **BREE: No, Bryony, we're not.** *(BRYONY hugs BREE, which the*
21   *latter tolerates. Then she takes her bag and the CD player,*
22   *and exits while BRYONY looks after her.)*

Thrown by Angels
by Gwendolyn Schwinke

Sissy — 18   Comic

Baby — 15

Baby has run away from their father's house and has been missing for two nights. When Baby and her sister were younger, they escaped with their father from a conflagration that destroyed their town, and in their escape they became separated from their mother. But for the past seven years their father has kept them locked in the basement, telling them the world was destroyed by fire, reading the Bible to them, and committing incest with both. This amusing scene is filled with discoveries as Baby excitedly reports to her sister what she has found outside their basement. On one level the situation appears very humorous, but on a much deeper level it will lead them to confront the nightmare of their relationship with their father and thrust them into a long and painful search for their own identities. See also a later scene from this play included in this section of scenes for two women.

1   BABY: It's out there.

2   SISSY: Baby, you're back, thank God. We thought you were

3   dead.

4   BABY: Did you hear me? It's out there.

5   SISSY: Daddy just left. He went out to look for you.

6   BABY: I know, I saw him go. I was hiding in the bushes.

7   SISSY: He's gonna be really mad about that.

8   BABY: I don't care, I don't care about him. Stop talking about

9   him. Listen to me: it is out there.

10 SISSY: What? What is out there?

11 BABY: The world! The whole world is out there.

12 SISSY: Well of course it's out there. The world has been burnt,

13   the world has been scorched, but it's still out there. It's not

1   like the fire ate away the whole planet and we're sitting on
2   some little chunk of rock hurtling through space.
3   BABY: No, I mean it's out there just like it was. Trees, grass,
4   birds ...
5   SISSY: Well, Baby, things grow back. Remember Noah? The
6   great flood? God's green earth will be renewed. That's the
7   whole point —
8   BABY: There's people.
9   SISSY: There are not.
10 BABY: Are too.
11 SISSY: You're telling me you saw people?
12 BABY: I did.
13 SISSY: Maybe they were angels. Or devils. Daddy told us long
14   ago, that after the fire angels and devils shall roam the
15   earth. It's a dangerous time. That was the very reason, in
16   case you forgot, that we were not supposed to leave the
17   basement. You just saw some devils. You're lucky they
18   didn't eat you up.
19 BABY: They gave me something.
20 SISSY: They did not ... What?
21 BABY: A cheeseburger.
22 SISSY: You are making that up!
23 BABY: And I ate it.
24 SISSY: You ate it? You ate food given you by devils? You're gonna
25   turn to stone or burst into flames or something.
26 BABY: They weren't devils, they were just regular people. They
27   were nice to me.
28 SISSY: Baby, what are you thinking with? The devil is always
29   nice. That's the way he operates.
30 BABY: Sissy, two nights ago when I ran off, I was so scared. You
31   know I haven't been out of this basement since we came
32   here seven years ago. But I couldn't help myself. That
33   night I looked over at him and I could not stand it, I could
34   not stand to be next to him, I could not stand to be in this
35   house any more. The window was open there in his room.

1   Just the screen was on it, and outside, I could see outside.

2   Upstairs there he has windows and some wind was

3   coming in and I could see some trees. He went to sleep,

4   and I just looked out that window, and smelled, and

5   listened. Something was out there. So I stood up on the

6   bed and I took a couple of big bounces, and I jumped right

7   at that screen. It crashed away, and I was out! I was on the

8   ground, and I just ran as fast as I could into the woods.

9   SISSY: I heard that, I was awake down here and I heard the

10   noise. Did he come after you? He did, didn't he?

11   BABY: He did, but out there the trees are thick, and I'm littler

12   than him. I'm faster, he couldn't catch me, and I just kept

13   running. He kept screaming that I wouldn't make it, that

14   the world was ended and I wouldn't last, but this thought

15   happened to me, Sissy, this thought –

16   SISSY: What?

17   BABY: This thought just popped into my head like something

18   you'd see in those little bubbles in the funny papers.

19   Remember that? Remember the funny papers? Where

20   people talk in bubbles? I don't know why I remembered

21   the bubbles, but I did, and this is the thing that was in my

22   bubble: To Hell With You! And then I said it out loud. And

23   I realized that it was a prayer. It's not a prayer you kneel

24   for – it's a prayer you pray when you're running. So for

25   hours and hours I ran, and I prayed: To Hell With You.

26   SISSY: Baby, that'll send you straight to hell.

27   BABY: Yeah, maybe, but listen to what happened. After a long

28   while I got too tired to run, and I got really too tired to

29   even be scared. I just went to sleep there on the ground, in

30   the dark. And when I woke up it was light – the sun was

31   coming up, and it was so beautiful. The sky was all purply-

32   blue and it was turning white over where the sun was ...

33   and I started looking around me and seeing all this stuff.

34   And that's when I realized: the world is still out there!

35   Trees and grass and wind and birds –

1   SISSY: Things grow back ...

2   BABY: These were big trees, I'm telling you, really old, big trees.

3   Older than seven years.

4   SISSY: It could have been a trick, a miracle ...

5   BABY: They were just regular old trees. I got up and I started

6   walking to the sun. I walked all day, until I got under

7   where the sun was in the sky, and I passed it up and kept

8   walking. About the time it got dark, I started to hear

9   noises. Frogs ...

10 SISSY: Oh, no ...

11 BABY: No, it was good, and then a whippoorwill! Remember

12   whippoorwills? I heard one, and then I heard this soft

13   rushing, like the wind, but different. So I followed the

14   sound, and then I saw a light, in the distance. It was

15   orange, and kind of glowing, and I went towards it.

16 SISSY: Baby, I know you're a genius and everything, but

17   sometimes you act like you don't have a brain in your head –

18 BABY: And when I got closer, there was less trees and the noise

19   was really loud, like a roaring –

20 SISSY: Oh, Baby, how could you do something as –

21 BABY: And it was a highway. With cars. And lights. And right

22   there by the highway, was my big orange glow. It was a

23   sign.

24 SISSY: A sign of the devil.

25 BABY: No. Burger King. *(Holds out a paper bag.)* I brought one

26   for you. I ate one, nothing happened to me. This one's

27   yours, a big, fat, flame-broiled Whopper. It took me a day

28   to remember my way back, so it's cold now, but you can

29   still smell it. I started out with some fries, too, but I

30   couldn't help myself.

31 SISSY: *(Unable to resist the temptation, she rips into the burger*

32   *and speaks with her mouth full.)* It's real! This is the real

33   thing!

34 BABY: The world isn't over. It's all out there. Hamburgers, cars,

35   people, television, music, computers. They still have it. It's

1   **just like it was before. He lied to us.**
2   **SISSY: He would never lie to us. Why would he lie? What earthly**
3   **reason would he have for lying to us about the end of the**
4   **world?**
5   **BABY: Sissy.** *(Pause.)* **There's boys.**
6   **SISSY: Boys?**
7   **BABY: Boys.** *(Short pause while SISSY considers this.)*
8   **SISSY: All right. Let's go!**

"By Looking"

from *The Pink Plays* by Kerri Kochanski

Ellie — 15   Comic

J — 15

*Ellie is a troublemaker, a little tougher than J, and somewhat
conceited. J usually follows Ellie's lead. This scene offers the actresses
a wonderful opportunity to play entirely to the audience as they stare
at and criticize "the girl" off-stage. When played successfully, by the
end of the scene the spectator should see the girl off-stage as clearly as
the on-stage characters do. Both Ellie and J are competing for the
attention of Conrad, captain of the football team, but Conrad's latest
interest seems to be the girl in question. The features to look for here
are the moments when each girl discovers something revealing about
herself as the dialog continues: do they dress like sluts, and what does
that mean? Do they need to adopt the image of those girls that the
boys have pinned up in their lockers? Are they very competitive with
each other even though they're "friends"? The scene also forces each
character to struggle now and then with a solution for some questions
they hadn't ever really considered before: how important are clothes
and makeup for their self-image? What do boys really want in a
girlfriend? Could either character conceive of herself with a different
public image? And there is ample opportunity in the scene for the
actresses to devise business, gestures, and movements to accompany
the action. The scene is high school: in the schoolyard, the gym, the
cafeteria. As the scene begins, the girls, wearing skimpy skirts, heavy
makeup, and big hair, are looking at the girl off-stage.*

1   J: Oh, is that her ... ?
2   ELLIE: From what I understand ... From what I'd guess ...
3   J: I didn't think she'd —
4   ELLIE: *(Quickly, jumping on top of it)* Why? What do you think
5   she'd —
6   J: I don't know. *(Beat.)* "Slight." She's "slight." I would think

1   she'd be more ... striking. Have more "oomph" to her. I
2   mean, to get Conrad, you'd have to have "oomph" ...
3   Wouldn't you think?
4   ELLIE: Not if Conrad wasn't looking for – I mean, Conrad ... he's
5   a guy ...
6   J: *(Stressing)* A guy ...
7   ELLIE: Yes, "a guy ..." *(She sits.)* But not like all the others ... For
8   some reason ... I mean, I've tried and tried.
9   J: I've seen you. I've seen you in action.
10 ELLIE: This skirt, these shoes ... I would think he would've
11   been into –
12 J: But not him.
13 ELLIE: For *some reason. (Looking)* He's into her ... Look at her:
14   she doesn't even have makeup on her face ... she doesn't
15   know how to comb her hair ... *(She begins to feel faux sick.)*
16   Maybe he goes for –
17 J: The natural look. *(ELLIE begins to feel increasingly weak.)*
18 ELLIE: Maybe he likes girls ...
19 J: Without lipstick, without hairspray – without all the things
20   we *need*, all the things we require to make us pretty. And
21   he goes for –
22 ELLIE: I just don't understand it ... Captain of the football team
23   ... You would think –
24 J: Maybe some guys don't think about –
25 ELLIE: But they see. They can *see* what's right in front of them,
26   can't they? They hang pictures – Jennifer Love Hewitt in
27   their lockers – you see her? You see her, don't you? With
28   her chest hanging out, with her makeup ... her long, back
29   eyelashes ... mascara all around. Don't you see it?
30 J: I see "it." *(She points to the girl and begins to shake her head.)*
31   And I just don't understand.
32 ELLIE: I don't understand. Me ... *(She begins to get upset.)* I'm
33   the one that spends the effort. I'm the one that tries hard
34   – look at me! I spent all my money ...
35 J: And Conrad ... he doesn't even notice.

1   ELLIE: Doesn't even care. *(Beat.)* **She's staring at us ... She's**
2   **staring at us, staring at her ...** *(Beat.)* **Don't look away ...**
3   J: I'm not looking away.
4   ELLIE: We'll stare her down.
5   J: Stare her down ... *(They stare at the girl. Beat.)*
6   ELLIE: She flinched. I knew she couldn't compete with us. And
7   she did. She flinched ...
8   J: Doesn't matter, though ...
9   ELLIE: What do you mean it doesn't matter? Of course it
10   matters. We are better than her. We are stronger. I could
11   go over there and kick her ass right now. I could go over
12   there and pound in her head. At least it would give her
13   some color. Getting blood on her cheeks. Then she'd be
14   able to see – *he'd* be able to see – what someone looks like.
15   When they are not pale and pasty. When they have some
16   "color," yes. Color to their character ... Doesn't she look –
17   J: She's laughing ... She's pointing to your skirt and laughing ...
18   ELLIE: I could go over there –
19   J: Don't.
20   ELLIE: But I *could*. I could go.
21   J: And you would start a fight. And then we'd get suspended.
22   ELLIE: *I'd* get suspended.
23   J: We'd *both* get suspended.
24   ELLIE: *(Still looking at the girl)* Why you?
25   J: Because friends have a way of getting mixed up in the trouble
26   of their friends ... and I really don't want ... I have a date on
27   Friday.
28   ELLIE: Anthony ... ? *(J doesn't respond.)* Don't tell me you're
29   going out with Anthony ... ? He said you were a –
30   J: I know what he said.
31   ELLIE: Then how? Why!?
32   J: He's ... not like Conrad ... *(ELLIE looks at her, doesn't*
33   *understand.)* He *likes* me ...
34   ELLIE: You have to go out with everyone who likes you?
35   J: There aren't that many.

1   **ELLIE: You could go out with Justin ... Mike —**
2   **J: Justin and Mike are —**
3   **ELLIE: What?**
4   **J: They don't keep their hands to themselves ... and I like**
5   **keeping their hands in one place.** *(ELLIE considers this.)*
6   **ELLIE: So take them off.**
7   **J: You can't just take off guys' hands ...**
8   **ELLIE: Why not?**
9   **J: Because they put them back on!**
10 **ELLIE:** *(Looking at J's short skirt)* **That skirt ...**
11 **J: Well, it's not like yours is any better ... I mean, it's not like you**
12   **have some *leverage* on the matter. I mean, your skirt is**
13   **higher but —**
14 **ELLIE:** *(Reiterating)* **"Higher." My skirt is "higher."**
15 **J:** *(Annoyed)* **So?**
16 **ELLIE:** *(Shrugs)* **Nothing. Just my skirt is higher.**
17 **J: So you think you're better than me? Just because your skirt is**
18   **—** *(ELLIE shrugs, but really believes she is better. J defends*
19   *herself.)* **My legs are shorter!** *(ELLIE shrugs again, knowing*
20   *she is better.)*
21 **ELLIE: And that, too ...**
22 **J: So just because ... just because I have shorter legs —**
23 **ELLIE: Why are you getting all upset about it? If you want**
24   **longer legs, just wear higher heels. Now, if I wear higher**
25   **heels, my legs, of course, will *still* be longer than yours.**
26   **But sometimes, if you want, I can wear low heels ...** *(She*
27   *decides.)* **I will wear low heels ...** *(Phony)* **Because I am your**
28   **friend! Because I want you to feel *good* about yourself ...**
29   *(Lying)* **Because we are *not* competing for Conrad ...** *(J looks*
30   *at the girl.)*
31 **J: She doesn't have high heels ... she doesn't have any heels ...**
32   *(She tries to see.)* **I don't think ...** *(She crouches down, trying*
33   *to see the girl's feet.)* **In fact, I think ... in fact, I think she is**
34   **wearing cowboy boots ...**
35 **ELLIE: Cowboy boots?**

1   J: Well, they *would* go with that skirt.
2   ELLIE: *(Speaking like nails grating on a chalkboard)* That *long*
3   skirt ... that very *long* skirt ...
4   J: It doesn't seem to bother Conrad. *(ELLIE makes a face and*
5   *wonders.)* So would you wear it ... ? Wear that skirt? If you
6   knew it would attract ... ?
7   ELLIE: I would *never* wear that skirt. Never ever — in a million
8   years!
9   J: But your goal —
10 ELLIE: Is not to change who I am. *(Gestures to her outfit.)* **This**
11   is me. *This* is who I am.
12 J: A slut?
13 ELLIE: I'm not a slut. I just dress like one.
14 J: So you think people will get "an idea"?
15 ELLIE: I think people will think I'm sexy.
16 J: But you're sexless — you're a virgin.
17 ELLIE: Virgins are allowed to dress slutty, too.
18 J: But you're not a slut.
19 ELLIE: I just dress like one.
20 J: Act.
21 ELLIE: Not "act." *Dress*.
22 J: Isn't it the same thing? Your dressing up —
23 ELLIE: Dressing up for me.
24 J: But you're misrepresenting yourself.
25 ELLIE: Because I can be however I want to be —
26 J: As long as it's not slutty.
27 ELLIE: I told you I'm not.
28 J: "Officially slutty."
29 ELLIE: Not a slut.
30 J: And officially a slut would be acting in the manner that a slut
31   would act, but not dressing like a slut herself —
32 ELLIE: Of course.
33 J: *(Turning to the girl)* So what is she ... if not a slut?
34 ELLIE: *(Considering the girl)* A "priss." It would appear to me
35   that she's a "priss."

1   J: But what if she doesn't *act* like a priss?

2   ELLIE: She acts like a priss.

3   J: She is *dressed* like a priss, but it doesn't mean that she

4   actually *is* one — a priss, I mean.

5   ELLIE: She's a priss ... *(She begins to vamp.)* She just doesn't

6   have the talent, the ambience ...

7   J: So Conrad likes prisses.

8   ELLIE: *(Feeling defeated)* I guess. *(Beat.)* I guess he likes ... what

9   I'm not.

10 J: A non-slut ...

11 ELLIE: Who looks like ...

12 J: A slut.

13 ELLIE: *(Exasperated, confused)* Who am I!? *(Considers herself.*

14   *Looks at her outfit.)* Do you think I look *too* slutty?

15 J: *(Considers herself.)* You're asking *me* ... ?

16 ELLIE: So you know you look like a —

17 J: Yeah. *(She pats her hair back into place, pleased that she looks*

18   *like a slut.)* It's what I'm going for.

19 ELLIE: *(Wondering if J is a slut)* So are you ... ?

20 J: What do you think?

21 ELLIE: Well, I would think, by looking ... *(She turns away from J,*

22   *not wanting to get into it.)* It's really none of my business ...

23 J: Looks can be deceiving. *(They continue to stand there.)*

24 ELLIE: *(Gesturing to the girl)* Looks can get Conrad.

25   *(Disheartened.)* Certain looks ... *(They stand, looking at the*

26   *girl.)* Where would you even *get* that skirt?

27 J: *(Wondering)* Does that mean you're getting it ... ?

28 ELLIE: *(Not understanding)* I *don't* get it ... I don't get it at *all.*

Jennie
by Meri Wallace

Sara — 15   Seriocomic
Jennie — 15

*This scene is wonderfully written to give actresses a chance to build a
very strong and compelling relationship in a very short time. It's also
a scene filled with discoveries that each makes about the other and
about themselves as their relationship unfolds. In addition to these
built-in features of dynamic development, there is ample opportunity
for the actresses to explore the physical space and the timing of their
dialog and physical movements; as well as their use of humor and
role-playing. As the scene begins, Sara enters with a flashlight and
stumbles over Jennie who is sitting on the ground.*

1   SARA: *(Shining a flashlight on JENNIE)* **Oh, god! You scared me.**
2   JENNIE: **I'm sorry.**
3   SARA: **No. I'm sorry I stepped on you. I didn't see you. Are you**
4   **OK?**
5   JENNIE: **I'm fine.**
6   SARA: **Have you been crying?**
7   JENNIE: **I must have gotten some dirt in my eyes.** *(She pushes*
8   *the flashlight away.)*
9   SARA: **What are you doing here anyway?**
10 JENNIE: **I'm trying to get away from my family. I needed some**
11   **time to be alone.**
12 SARA: **I can understand that. Mine drives me crazy, too. I'm**
13   **Sara.**
14 JENNIE: **Jennie.**
15 SARA: *(Looking at JENNIE's backpack)* **Are you going**
16   **somewhere?**
17 JENNIE: **Oh ... just some stuff I was going to wash in the**
18   **bathroom.**

1   **SARA: Isn't it kind of late at night for that?**
2   **JENNIE: Avoid the morning rush? Look, I'd better be going.**
3   **SARA: No, wait. I didn't mean to snoop. Please don't go.** *(They*
4   *sit on a bench.)* **Where's your campsite?**
5   **JENNIE:** *(Pointing)* **We're in an ugly rented tent over there.**
6   **SARA: Mine is that huge white camper by the office, with that**
7   **ridiculous pink and white striped awning, and the**
8   **gigantic flag sticking out the back.**
9   **JENNIE: Oh, yes, I've seen that one.** *(They laugh.)*
10 **SARA: It's so embarrassing. How long are you here until?**
11 **JENNIE: I'll be here for awhile.**
12 **SARA: You're lucky. We're only here until Sunday. It's so great**
13   **to get away from the city. It's been so hot and humid. All**
14   **my friends are away anyway. I love being in the woods, but**
15   **to tell you the truth, sometimes I wish we were going**
16   **home tomorrow. My older brother is so annoying. He**
17   **sleeps near me and is always sticking his big smelly feet in**
18   **my face.**
19 **JENNIE: Brothers are such a pain. My two younger brothers**
20   **snore all night long. And when it's hot and humid and**
21   **you're already tossing and turning, you hear ...** *(She makes*
22   *snoring sounds)* **... it makes it even harder to fall asleep. I**
23   **feel like killing them most of the time.**
24 **SARA: The thing I miss most here is instant-messaging my**
25   **friends. My parents wouldn't let me bring my computer**
26   **along. You know, "family time."** *(She makes quotation signs*
27   *with her fingers.)* **Do you have a computer?**
28 **JENNIE: No, I don't.**
29 **SARA: Damn. Did they make you leave yours at home, too?**
30 **JENNIE: This is my home.** *(SARA is shocked and perplexed.)*
31 **SARA: What do you mean?**
32 **JENNIE: I live here.**
33 **SARA: You live here?**
34 **JENNIE: We can't afford to pay for a house during the summer.**
35   **It's too expensive. But we'll probably look for a place at the**

1   end of September.
2   SARA: I can't imagine that. A week, but several months? Never.
3   The showers only have cold water. It's so yucky when it
4   rains. What do you do all day?
5   JENNIE: It certainly isn't about riding bicycles and enjoying the
6   "great" outdoors. We have to collect wood for the fire at
7   night. We have to keep our tent clean. That way we won't
8   have sand in it. We have to make sure that we're clean and
9   that our sheets are aired out. That way it all stays fresh. My
10   dad always says, "We have to keep everything together.
11   Otherwise everything could fall apart."
12   SARA: God. I feel awful for you. I couldn't live with my family
13   in such tight quarters for that long. Was that why you were
14   crying before?
15   JENNIE: Yes. My mom and I don't get along. She's the bossy
16   kind. When I sweep the tent it's never good enough.
17   Tonight it was my middle brother's turn to wash the
18   dishes. He refused, so my mother said I had to do it. It's so
19   unfair. I always have to do everything. I can't stand it. OK.
20   That's enough. I've already said too much. I'm going.
21   SARA: Don't go. *(JENNIE hesitates and turns to listen.)* Me and
22   my mom are having problems, too. We actually had a huge
23   fight and I refused to go. They forced me to come along
24   camping. I'm really mad at her. There's this boy. His name
25   is Alex, and I really like him. But my mom doesn't want
26   me to have a boyfriend. I don't know why. When Alex calls,
27   she picks up an extension and listens to our
28   conversations. After a few minutes she interrupts us and
29   tells me I have to hang up. I want to be with him, but she
30   won't let me. Can I tell you something I haven't told
31   anybody?
32   JENNIE: Sure.
33   SARA: Alex doesn't go to my school. We've started cutting
34   classes to see each other. We hang out here and there. Now
35   my mom is furious because my grades are dropping. She's

1   taken away my TV and grounded me for life. All I have
2   now is my computer. Soon she'll take that away, too. I'm
3   afraid she'll stop me from seeing him altogether. I can't
4   stand her.
5 JENNIE: Do you love Alex?
6 SARA: Yes, I do.
7 JENNIE: I never had a real boyfriend, but I once liked a boy a
8   whole lot. He was camping like we were, but he moved to
9   a different campground. I never saw him again.
10 SARA: Do you think we'll get along with our moms when we're
11   grown up? Like those daughters who go shopping with
12   their moms and are their best friends?
13 JENNIE: Tonight, I heard my mom crying in the dark. Her life
14   is so hard. I feel so bad that I hurt her. Sometimes I think
15   she'd be better off without me around.
16 SARA: My friends keep me going when things are rough.
17 JENNIE: I really don't have any. Sometimes I make new friends
18   here, but then they leave.
19 SARA: Without my friends I'd have no life. Maybe you and I
20   could be friends.
21 JENNIE: You're leaving soon.
22 SARA: Well, we can hang out until I leave.
23 JENNIE: Maybe. *(Pause.)*
24 SARA: Do you Rollerblade? I brought mine along.
25 JENNIE: No. But I love playing sports. There was basketball at
26   school, but it was on Mondays, and every Monday we have
27   to rent another campsite, because we're only allowed a
28   one-week stay. Softball is all the way in Patchogue, and
29   there's no one to take me. I only made it to two games, that
30   was it.
31 SARA: Couldn't your dad bring you?
32 JENNIE: Yes, but he isn't around much. He works two jobs. One
33   in maintenance at a hotel in Amagansett and one at a
34   garage in Hampton Bays. He's so tired all the time.
35 SARA: Why don't you come over to my camper and we'll hang

1   out tomorrow.

2 JENNIE: I may not be here.

3 SARA: I thought you were staying for a few months.

4 JENNIE: I'm leaving tonight.

5 SARA: What do you mean? Are you ... running away? Where will

6   you go?

7 JENNIE: To the city.

8 SARA: Where in the city? Do you know anyone?

9 JENNIE: No. Maybe I'll go to a shelter. At least there'll be a roof

10   over my head.

11 SARA: Yeah. But they're crazy places. People stab each other

12   and everything. And what would you do for money?

13 JENNIE: I'll find a way. I can't stand being here and poor

14   anymore. *(A voice calls from Off-stage: "Sara.")*

15 SARA: That's my mom.

16 JENNIE: You better go.

17 SARA: Do your parents know about this? You need to talk to

18   them. You could get hurt in the city. *("Sara," a voice calls*

19   *out more insistently.)*

20 JENNIE: You better go. It sounds like your mom is starting to

21   get upset.

22 SARA: Come with me.

23 JENNIE: I can't.

24 SARA: Come over to my camper. We could hang out there and

25   talk some more.

26 JENNIE: Your mom is going to flip.

27 SARA: No, really, I mean it. Come with me. *(SARA's mom calls*

28   *again.)*

29 JENNIE: You better answer her.

30 SARA: *(Calling towards the voice)* **Mom! By the bathroom! I'll be**

31   **right there!** *(JENNIE grabs her stuff and exits. SARA turns*

32   *back and realizes that JENNIE has gone.)* **Jennie! Jennie!**

Donny's Diner
by Shirley King

Lulu — 20s   **Comic**
Dana — 20s

This scene challenges the actresses to sustain brisk and lively repartee throughout. Dana and Lulu are old friends — perhaps from girlhood — and the situation allows the actresses to build an imaginary biography around each character. The dialog is perfectly structured — as is the scenic action — to reach a clear climax in the last few pages and lead each character to make a variety of discoveries, a number of conclusions, and a range of decisions about her life. There is also a running-bit of comic tension throughout since the scene is frequently propelled by Dana's ravenous appetite as she ineffectually tries to summon the waiter. Finally, the scene leaves it up to the actresses to decide whether anything of any importance at all is touched upon by the two women's conversation: is this just another lunch date conversation, or will Dana and Lulu really embark on a new course following their chat? At the beginning of the scene Dana is sitting at a table in Donny's Diner, writing in a notebook, when Lulu enters.

1   LULU: OK, I did it, Dana. Darryl and I are so over.
2   DANA: About time. Sit down and let's order.
3   LULU: What's that you're doing?
4   DANA: Figuring out a math problem. See, you take the
5   logarithm, base ten, of each side of the equals sign and
6   then apply the properties of logarithms — well, I can do
7   this later. You and Darryl broke up because of Elvis?
8   LULU: Look, sometimes I do see Elvis, OK?
9   DANA: Not OK. You need to stop seeing dead people. Know what
10   I'd like while we're waiting? Cheez Doodles.
11   LULU: You said that last time.
12   DANA: So now I can't ever say "Cheez Doodles" again? All right,

1   what happened with Darryl?

2   LULU: I told him, "Get out of my life."

3   DANA: Good for you. So what happened?

4   LULU: Well, he didn't respect me. Want to watch the lunar

5   eclipse tonight?

6   DANA: The one where you go blind? I don't think so.

7   LULU: That's the solar eclipse. Lunar's ... well, I'm not sure. But

8   you might need binoculars. Know what Darryl said right

9   after I told him off?

10 DANA: Darryl said something? Who knew he could speak?

11 LULU: Darryl said, "Fine with me. I've got someone else I'm

12   dating anyways."

13 DANA: Someone left half a hoagie on that plate over there.

14   Unbelievable.

15 LULU: Sit down, Dana.

16 DANA: Look, this is serious. I missed breakfast and I'm

17   starving.

18 LULU: Dana, I said sit down. When I dumped Darryl he all of a

19   sudden said he felt like smashing my face. Guess what I

20   told him.

21 DANA: "Try that, Darryl, and you end up wearing an orange

22   jumpsuit." Waitress?

23 LULU: Try "server" or "waitperson."

24 DANA: I am not yelling "server" or "waitperson." That's just

25   plain dumb.

26 LULU: But you will, you always do. FYI, I did see Elvis. Dressed-

27   down for casual Friday, looking cool. Khakis, Doc

28   Martens, plaid shirt open at the neck, wearing that teal

29   silk scarf.

30 DANA: How'd you know it was Elvis?

31 LULU: Oh, please. I just *knew*, that's all. He served time in the

32   Army, you know. Join the Army, you get a signing bonus.

33   That's what Darryl said.

34 DANA: And these days a military funeral. Waitress? Waitress!

35   You know the odds of getting served here?

1   LULU: No, do you? Oh, right, of course, you do. You got an "A" in
2   Statistics. Are you coming over to see the eclipse?
3   DANA: That same eclipse I just said "no" to? Could I eat this
4   horseradish?
5   LULU: Not without water from the waitperson. My phone's
6   vibrating. Hello? Oh ... Darryl. Speaking of. Can't live
7   without me, huh? OK, tell me – I know you're dying to ...
8   what's her name? *(To Dana:)* Shaneesha.
9   DANA: I think I know her. Spiky green hair, three piercings?
10 LULU: *(On the phone)* OK. Nice name. See, I'm good with that.
11   Kimberly or Dawn or Liz ... but no, Shaneesha I can live
12   with.
13 DANA: If that waitperson isn't here in two minutes, I'm raiding
14   the kitchen.
15 LULU: *(Still on the phone)* So what's her number? I've got some
16   information she might need. Yeah, about you. OK? *(LULU*
17   *clicks the phone off.)* What next? When do I see the white
18   elephant?
19 DANA: Next week at Holy Redeemer. My Aunt Teri's in charge.
20 LULU: Not the church bazaar. I mean the white elephant Elvis
21   kept wanting to buy for Graceland but never could find.
22   It's a fact. He kept searching and searching –
23 DANA: Why is this important?
24 LULU: We're all searching for something, Dana. With Elvis it
25   was an elephant. With me, it's making something good
26   out of my life. Oops, my phone again. Darryl? You are so
27   busted, Darryl. I don't need you in my life. Don't ever call
28   me again, OK? *(LULU clicks off phone.)* See, Darryl and I
29   were on the way out soon as I started having my singing
30   career, which he hated – you know? But then I kept
31   running into Elvis who was so encouraging. He kept
32   saying, "That's all right, mama. Keep on singing, darlin'."
33 DANA: Don't you think it's time you got over Elvis? He'd be way
34   too old for you by now.
35 LULU: No, no. Elvis Aaron Presley, born – I know this. 1935,

1 '36? O-my-god. He's what — seventy?

2 DANA: You didn't notice when you saw him?

3 LULU: He started coloring his hair real young — OK? And then

4 the neck scarf hid the chins. Also he's got that full face, so

5 the wrinkles don't show. But never mind that. He's still

6 king of my heart.

7 DANA: Yeah, but seventy?

8 LULU: Omigod — my phone again.

9 DANA: *(Grabs the phone.)* Darryl? Lulu's sick of you and so am I.

10 Oh, Mrs. Jackson. Yes, she's here. *(To LULU)* Your Mom.

11 LULU: Hi, Mom. Not much. What're *you* doing? Sure, I'll be

12 home for dinner. What're we having? Mac and Cheese?

13 Cool. Bye, Mom.

14 DANA: I'm coming, too. That's the only way I'll ever get any

15 food.

16 LULU: OK, Dana, here's the drill. Tonight we're gonna stand at

17 the window watching the earth's shadow cover the

18 moon's face *or* the moon passing over the humungous

19 earth and then Elvis will show himself. He will be leading

20 a white elephant on a gold leash. Guess what I'm telling

21 Elvis when I see him?

22 DANA: That you're hot for dead rock stars. You worry me, girl.

23 Can't you just get over it and move on? How much singing

24 are you doing anyway? When's your next gig?

25 LULU: Elks Club benefit. I mostly sing for charity. Last time it

26 was earthquakes. You don't even know what do in an

27 earthquake, do you?

28 DANA: Scream and run.

29 LULU: See, that is so wrong. So is duck and cover. You need to

30 get close to the biggest thing around, like a bed or a couch.

31 There's this safety space, like a magic bubble. Elvis, he's a

32 total chunk, but I'm not thinking of him as a safety space;

33 that would be taking advantage. What's that sound?

34 DANA: My stomach. Can you read the headlines? Dana Hawkins

35 dies of hunger in Donny's Diner. *(Yells.)* Waitress?

1   Waitperson? Server?

2 LULU: See? You yelled it. My opinion, Dana? You're not looking

3   at this right. We're all put here to give of ourselves, like me

4   and my singing and Elvis and his. Seems like you, you're

5   just here on earth to get.

6 DANA: Lulu, it's a diner – I'm here to get food. Aren't you?

7 LULU: Me? I'm just here to see what's up with you.

8 DANA: OK, that's it. *(DANA grabs LULU's cell phone.)* Operator?

9   Give me the Pizza Pirate Café. Hello, Pirate? One super-

10   size pizza. Deep dish, fine. Marinara, fine. Artichoke

11   hearts, anchovies, fine with me.

12 LULU: No anchovies. You need to watch your salt intake. Salt

13   makes you retain water.

14 DANA: *(Still on phone)* Delivered? You bet. Right now, to

15   Donny's Diner. *(To LULU)* When my pizza gets here, I'm

16   sharing with you. Get it? That's *me* giving to *you*, making

17   me a *giving* person. And about me saying the same stuff

18   over and over, when will you get off Elvis and that asinine

19   eclipse?

20 LULU: OK, you're sharing. That's really good. Even if you're all

21   bent about it. And you know, this eclipse and Elvis, well,

22   they're harmless – right? I'm not hurting anyone. So

23   what's your problem?

24 DANA: You know, I don't know.

25 LULU: I did what I needed to. Got rid of Darryl, who didn't

26   respect me, and now I'm gonna keep singing. So what are

27   you doing to be happy? Anything?

28 DANA: Nothing. I'm not thinking happy. I don't have a clue. Or

29   even a dream. At least you've got one.

30 LULU: Well, tonight you can share the eclipse with me and then

31   who knows? Maybe you'll find a dream, too. You're good at

32   lots of things.

33 DANA: Like, for example, what?

34 LULU: Take the big picture: you've got math and statistics. How

35   many people are good at those?

1 DANA: Math's easy.
2 LULU: Dana, math is not easy. You could be a total math genius.
3   You know? You could even —
4 DANA: Teach. I keep thinking that. But do I want to sit at a desk
5   all day long?
6 LULU: My math teachers didn't sit. They were up and down at
7   the blackboard, they walked, they talked, they even left
8   the room while we did problems.
9 DANA: Yeah, mine, too. I finished the tests way before the other
10   kids and then didn't even have the teacher to talk to. He
11   was out having a smoke.
12 LULU: See, you write a book about math and then you go on
13   Oprah and then they make a movie of your book and you
14   get to donate money to charities. And you could also be
15   helping people with their taxes. Wouldn't that be good?
16 DANA: Know what else? I could tell them where their tax dollar
17   goes.
18 LULU: You know that, too? You are so smart. Where?
19 DANA: Out of every dollar, forty-two cents goes for war,
20   seventeen cents for Medicaid: that's medical care and
21   nursing homes for old people and disabled —
22 LULU: That's all? Just seventeen cents?
23 DANA: Sixteen cents for running the government, ten cents for
24   the national debt, nine cents for education, job training
25   and social services, two cents for protecting the
26   government —
27 LULU: That is so wrong. What people need to do is change this.
28   That could be your dream.
29 DANA: Or not.
30 LULU: Look at it this way: there's more of us — meaning more
31   and more people who care. What we all need to do is stand
32   up and keep standing up. We can do this. I know we can.
33 DANA: If it'll get you off Elvis, OK. I guess I can do some
34   standing up, or whatever.
35 LULU: No whatevers. We've got rights, you know.

1   DANA: Yeah, I'm good with that. So let's go outside and wait for
2   the pizza.
3   LULU: What're you bringing tonight to share, while we watch
4   the eclipse? Don't say leftover pizza, because we won't be
5   having any. I'll be lucky to get one slice.
6   DANA: I wasn't even thinking about pizza.
7   LULU: What, then?
8   DANA: Cheez Doodles?

Cell Cycle
by Cristina Pippa

Alicia — 19   **Seriocomic**
Caitlyn — 16

The following scene deftly tracks a growing sense of bonding between two sisters. Alicia, the older, really does care for Caitlyn, despite the latter's failure as a caregiver. As the scene develops, Alicia comes to realize how much her sister's religious feelings are grounded in the pain of loss that stretches back to the time when Caitlyn was just a little girl. Although Alicia criticizes Caitlyn's apparent indifference and satirizes her sentimental religious feelings, she recognizes her childlike need for comfort. Perhaps Alicia's realization also gives her pause to think about her own preoccupation with science and her emerging role as the older sister giving support to others. In the original production, Alicia is preparing dinner when Caitlyn enters carrying a purse and her Bible. See also a later scene from this play included in this section of scenes for two women.

1   CAITLYN: Have I been mean lately? I feel like I've been mean
2   lately.
3   ALICIA: I don't know.
4   CAITLYN: 'Cause we're all sinners, and I know I'm never going
5   to be perfect.
6   ALICIA: I didn't say you did anything.
7   CAITLYN: I just — can you give me grace?
8   ALICIA: I never say grace.
9   CAITLYN: I mean I want to ask for your forgiveness.
10 ALICIA: Sure. You've got it.
11 CAITLYN: Are you OK?
12 ALICIA: I guess I'm a little down. Like I just watched *Mystic*
13   *Pizza* or something.

1   CAITLYN: It was on TV?

2   ALICIA: No. I didn't watch it. I just feel like I did.

3   CAITLYN: *Mystic Pizza*'s not depressing. You're thinking of

4   *Saint Elmo's Fire.*

5   ALICIA: Have you seen *Mystic Pizza*? They're totally different.

6   CAITLYN: We should watch *Troop Beverly Hills*. That'll cheer

7   you up! Remember when we used to watch it all the time?

8   Now we're leaving such busy lives. We hardly get to see

9   each other.

10 ALICIA: Leading. I think the expression is "leading busy lives."

11 CAITLYN: Leaving, too. We're leaving sooner than we think.

12   But it's OK. Some people really worry about death. But

13   we're not so much dying as leaving. Leaving this strange

14   place where people fight and sin – to go home.

15 ALICIA: Why are you telling me this?

16 CAITLYN: I know you're really worried about Dad.

17 ALICIA: You're not?

18 CAITLYN: Of course. But also not.

19 ALICIA: It must be nice to have so little weighing you down.

20 CAITLYN: 'Cause God wants us to give all our cares to him, to let

21   him carry our burdens. Dad should do that. And you

22   should, too, Alicia. *(She waits for a response.)* I could help

23   you.

24 ALICIA: I'm almost finished.

25 CAITLYN: I mean help you find God.

26 ALICIA: Yeah, you're so helpful. Why didn't you take Dad to the

27   doctor so he wouldn't have to go by himself?

28 CAITLYN: He always goes by himself.

29 ALICIA: This was a bigger deal.

30 CAITLYN: I had Bible study with my friends. He said it was fine.

31   And you weren't there.

32 ALICIA: I'm working!

33 CAITLYN: It's no wonder you're depressed. You don't have God

34   and you're working in a morgue.

35 ALICIA: Next to a morgue. I'm working in a lab.

1   CAITLYN: Whatever.

2   ALICIA: And since you're not working, you should take care of

3   Dad. Spend time with him. Get him to go out to lunch.

4   CAITLYN: You're right. I haven't done as much as I should.

5   *(Pause, while she thinks.)* You know, there was a guy who

6   made it his goal to think about God as much as possible.

7   It's really hard. Even when I jog, I end up thinking about

8   what I'm going to wear when I go out.

9   ALICIA: But you do think of God all the time.

10 CAITLYN: I try.

11 ALICIA: To the point where you might be missing things

12   because he's —

13 CAITLYN: Missing what?

14 ALICIA: Anything. God's all you think about and whenever

15   you're not thinking of him, you're thinking about not

16   thinking of him, which means you're still thinking of him.

17 CAITLYN: Don't you think about science all the time?

18 ALICIA: Ummmm. Well, I do a lot, but I'm not sure as intensely.

19   Maybe.

20 CAITLYN: God and church and Young Life — they're just as

21   important to me. I know they're not to you.

22 ALICIA: Yeah, and they never were. That's what I wonder

23   about. Is it true there's a God gene?

24 CAITLYN: What's that?

25 ALICIA: A gene that makes you more likely to be religious?

26   Some geneticists say they've found it.

27 CAITLYN: I don't think so.

28 ALICIA: Then why do you think we have such ... different

29   beliefs? We had the same parents.

30 CAITLYN: I know why I need God. Sometimes I wish you did,

31   too, but I know that everyone has their moment.

32 ALICIA: You remember a moment? *(CAITLYN nods.)* When was

33   it?

34 CAITLYN: When I found out Mom was sick and was probably

35   going to die. I was little, but I still remember. I lay down

1   on that fuzzy rug in my room and I just cried and cried
2   and cried. You couldn't stop me.
3 ALICIA: I remember that.
4 CAITLYN: And it was Sunday, so Mom took me to the youth
5   group that night. I'd been there before, but I never ... I just
6   remember all these kids being so happy to see me. And
7   one of them had just lost her dad. You know Sarah
8   Brendan? Her dad had a heart attack at work, and her
9   mom was the youth minister and was so nice to me. She
10   was like Super Mom, you know? I even thought maybe
11   she'd marry Dad some day.
12 ALICIA: Ewwww.
13 CAITLYN: Yeah, that was dumb. She was kind of old. But I just
14   felt like everything was OK that night. That if God needed
15   Mom like he needed Sarah's dad, that would be OK with
16   me. Suddenly the world made sense.
17 ALICIA: I can see that.

Skid Marks II: Are We There Yet?
by Lindsay Price

Officer Emma — 20s   **Comic**
Connie — 18

This scene is taken from a play about road trip adventures. Connie is trying to change her life, but life has clearly overwhelmed her at this point in the drama. She is in the process of driving across the country to start school. As the scene begins, she's sitting in the front seat of her car and has just been pulled over. This short scene is very compressed, forcing the two actresses to explore the fun of fast character development, discoveries, and change — for the characters do change radically from beginning to end. Connie moves from near-hysteria at the outset to joy and celebration at the conclusion, and Officer Emma gradually sheds her hard-bitten exterior and becomes a co-conspirator by letting Connie drive off to claim her freedom. The actresses should decide where the major reversal occurs in the scene's structure in order to bring about this absurd character change. The key to this comic scene lies in playing a clear beginning-middle-end to the encounter.

1   CONNIE: Oh no, oh no, oh no, oh no, oh no, oh no, oh no, oh, no.
2   Oh no. Oh no. Get a grip, Connie. Get a grip. You didn't do
3   anything wrong. Breathe and smile. Breathe and smile.
4   Don't freak out. Don't faint. And don't throw up.
5   OFFICER EMMA: *(Approaching the car)* License and registration,
6   please.
7   CONNIE: *(To OFFICER EMMA)* I am not going to throw up.
8   OFFICER EMMA: License and registration, please.
9   CONNIE: I was doing the speed limit. I was doing the speed
10   limit. I'm not sure what the perception was of what I was
11   doing, but I was doing the speed limit.
12 OFFICER EMMA: License and registration, please.

1   CONNIE: Sure. No problem. Here you are. Everything hunky-
2   dory. No vomiting. No sir-ee. *(Looking at OFFICER EMMA)*
3   Uh ... Ma'am-ee.
4   OFFICER EMMA: Now, Ms. Killoran —
5   CONNIE: Connie. Call me Connie.
6   OFFICER EMMA: Now, Connie —
7   CONNIE: Do you have a name? Of course, you have a name.
8   What a stupid question. Never mind. "Officer" will suit
9   you just fine, right? And so it should. Who am I to ask your
10   name? *(Slaps herself on the wrist.)* Bad Connie! Not that I
11   speak about myself in the third person all the time. That's
12   weird. And I'm far from weird. Ha. *(OFFICER EMMA*
13   *shakes her head and looks like she's holding back a laugh.*
14   *She softens up.)*
15   OFFICER EMMA: Folks call me Officer Emma.
16   CONNIE: Emma, what a pretty name. *(She clears her throat.)* It's
17   a very tough, suitable name for a woman, person of the
18   law.
19   OFFICER EMMA: Do you know how fast you were going?
20   CONNIE: I wasn't going fast at all. That's my whole point. I'm
21   very careful to follow the rules of the road.
22   OFFICER EMMA: You were doing thirty-five.
23   CONNIE: Oh.
24   OFFICER EMMA: On a highway.
25   CONNIE: Is that bad?
26   OFFICER EMMA: Honey, you have to keep up with the other
27   cars. It's just as dangerous to go too slow as it is to go too
28   fast.
29   CONNIE: Right. I knew that. I see what you're saying.
30   Completely. Totally. Wholly. Spherically. Ha.
31   OFFICER EMMA: You've never been on the highway before,
32   have you?
33   CONNIE: Sure, I have. I absolutely have. Drive it all the time.
34   Every day, back and forth, zip, zip, zip.
35   OFFICER EMMA: Look me in the eye and say that.

1 CONNIE: There's a first time for everything, right?

2 OFFICER EMMA: Not when it's going to be your last.

3 CONNIE: You can't kick me off the highway! I'm not even

4   halfway there!

5 OFFICER EMMA: I'm sorry, honey, but —

6 CONNIE: Officer Emma, wait, just a second. Wait. *(She takes a*

7   *deep breath.)* Do you like peanut butter?

8 OFFICER EMMA: Not really. It sticks to the roof of my mouth.

9 CONNIE: That's what it does.

10 OFFICER EMMA: And crunchy's unpredictable. I always bite

11   down wrong on a peanut.

12 CONNIE: Officer, Emma, I have eaten peanut butter

13   sandwiches every day for four years. Ten years! Ever since

14   I can remember. It's not because I love peanut butter. I

15   don't. It's just there. Right in front of me. It's easy. It's easy

16   and once you get into that rut you can't get out. I am stuck

17   in a peanut butter rut. Do you know what that's like,

18   Officer Emma?

19 OFFICER EMMA: Umm-hmm. I know all about the rut. Peanut

20   butter rut, jujube rut, chocolate chip rut — they're all the

21   same.

22 CONNIE: It's not even unpredictable crunchy. It's flat, boring,

23   smooth, stick to the roof of your mouth, and I'm tired of

24   it, Officer Emma. I'm tired.

25 OFFICER EMMA: You have to put the peanut butter down.

26   Leave it be. Throw it out.

27 CONNIE: That's what I'm trying to do! I'm trying to change

28   everything in one fell swoop: peanut butter, school, life,

29   the whole ball of wax. Maybe it was too much to do all at

30   once —

31 OFFICER EMMA: You can't do these things in stages. It's all at

32   once or nothing.

33 CONNIE: So if I'm only going thirty-five on the highway, it's because

34   my brain is pretty much fried, I'm trying to get unstuck. I'm

35   trying to get peanut butter out of my life for good!

1   OFFICER EMMA: You go, girl! You go!

2   CONNIE: Thank you. You're so kind. Officer Emma, I know

3   what I was doing wrong, and I know you have a job to do,

4   but if you'll let me continue on, I promise, I solemnly vow

5   I'll keep up with the other cars.

6   OFFICER EMMA: You won't have to.

7   CONNIE: What? Why?

8   OFFICER EMMA: I'm giving you a police escort. As long as

9   you're in my jurisdiction, I'm going to get you all the help

10   you need. You can tell that nasty stuff that Officer Emma

11   is on the case. *(OFFICER EMMA exits.)*

12 CONNIE: Thank you, Officer Emma! Thank you! And I swear, as

13   long as I'm living, I'll never eat peanut butter again!

Thrown by Angels
by Gwendolyn Schwinke

Sissy — 18   Serious
Baby — 15

Sissy and Baby have run away from their father's house, and they are alone outside at night. When they were younger, they escaped with him from a conflagration that destroyed their town, and in their escape they became separated from their mother. But for the past seven years their father has kept them locked in the basement, telling them the world was destroyed by fire, reading to them from the Bible, and committing incest with them both. At this point in the women's story, they are venturing into a world of devastating revelations, interconnected lives, and strange new possibilities. And in this scene, they confront the reality of their sexual relationship with their father for the first time. See also the first scene from this play included in this section of two-women scenes.

1   SISSY: Find some little sticks
2   BABY: There's no little sticks here.
3   SISSY: It's outside, there have to be little sticks. You're just not
4   looking hard enough.
5   BABY: It's pretty hard to see little-bitsy sticks when it's pitch
6   black.
7   SISSY: Well, if we had little sticks for a fire, it wouldn't be pitch
8   black, so why don't you find some? Feel for them or
9   something.
10 BABY: Oh sure, and feel for broken glass. Bugs. Snakes.
11 SISSY: There's no snakes.
12 BABY: How do you know, Miss Know-it-all? How do you know
13   there's no snakes?
14 SISSY: There's no snakes here, it's practically a desert.
15 BABY: There's snakes in the desert.

1 SISSY: Not this one.

2 BABY: How do you know?

3 SISSY: Just find some sticks. Make a lot of noise, then if there

4 are any snakes, you'll scare them away. *(BABY begins to*

5 *look again, lighting matches to illuminate her search.*

6 *Occasionally she finds a small stick that she throws in the*

7 *direction of the fire.)*

8 BABY: Here. Here.

9 SISSY: Don't waste the matches.

10 BABY: I'm using the matches to find sticks. *(Tossing a stick)*

11 Here.

12 SISSY: Well, stop it. We can't afford to waste matches.

13 BABY: We have a ton of matches. I got some more at that last

14 place.

15 SISSY: Let me see. *(BABY digs in her pockets and brings out*

16 *fistfuls of matchbooks. She drops them all on the fire with*

17 *resulting bursts of flame.)* You idiot! What did you do that

18 for? *(SISSY tries to rescue matchbooks from the fire. Fails.)*

19 BABY: We can get some more. Every truck stop we've been at

20 had matches, matches, matches. The world is swimming

21 in matches.

22 SISSY: Yeah, well great. I guess we'd better hitch another ride,

23 then, because you just burned up our entire supply. *(BABY*

24 *pulls out a lighter, flicks it.)* Where'd you get that?

25 BABY: From the last man that gave us a ride.

26 SISSY: You stole it?

27 BABY: He won't care. *(She flicks the lighter for emphasis.)* He had

28 another one right there in his truck. You can get fire

29 everywhere, there is no shortage of fire.

30 SISSY: You can't think like that. You can't take things for

31 granted. You can't be too careful about your own survival.

32 BABY: You sound like Dad.

33 SISSY: I do not.

34 BABY: "You can't be too careful about your own survival."

35 "Waste not, want not." "You are the hope of the world."

1   SISSY: Why don't you just keep quiet and look for more sticks?
2   BABY: "You are the last remaining repository of the human
3   gene pool."
4   SISSY: Shut up!
5   BABY: And you believed him! You fell for it.
6   SISSY: How was I supposed to know?
7   BABY: Yeah, well, when I went upstairs to him, at least I had
8   enough sense to look out the window.
9   SISSY: I looked out the window!
10 BABY: You did? The first night when you went up there, you
11   looked out the window?
12 SISSY: Of course I did.
13 BABY: And what did you see?
14 SISSY: I saw trees tossing themselves around. Whips of
15   lightning snapping through the sky and they almost hit
16   the trees, but the trees bent to get out of the way. First it
17   was night, then day, then night again – it changed every
18   second. Finally there was a huge noise – the loudest noise
19   I've ever heard in my life – and the sky opened up. When
20   it opened the rain came out – I could smell the rain. And
21   I thought, this is God's rain, God's tears for my child
22   conceived in sorrow. It's a sign, my child conceived in rain
23   will be born under a bow like God sent to Noah. My child
24   will be a new start, the hope of the world.
25 BABY: You liked it! You liked being in his house and in his bed!
26 SISSY: I left, didn't I?
27 BABY: I hate you.
28 SISSY: Well, maybe you'd be better off without me then.
29 BABY: Maybe I would.
30 SISSY: Just try it, I'd like to see how long you'd last on your own.
31   You can't even start a fire.
32 BABY: Oh, that's so hard. Gee, how will I ever start a fire! *(She*
33   *flicks her lighter, throws it up, catches it, stuffs it in her*
34   *pocket.)* **Good luck, Matchless.** *(She starts to leave.)*
35 SISSY: Baby, wait. Can't we talk?

1　BABY: Sure. What do you want to talk about? I know — how
2　　　about the Bible? I haven't heard a Bible verse in months.
3　　　Will you recite for me, Sissy? Genesis nineteen, verse
4　　　thirty through thirty-six.
5　SISSY: "Now Lot went up out of Zoar, and dwelt in the hills with
6　　　his two daughters, for he was afraid to dwell in Zoar; so he
7　　　dwelt in a cave with his two daughters. And the first-born
8　　　said to the younger, 'Our father is old and there is not a
9　　　man on earth to come in to us after the manner of all the
10　　　earth. Come, let us make our father drink wine, and we
11　　　will lie with him, that we may preserve offspring through
12　　　our father.' So they made their father drink wine that
13　　　night; and the first-born went in and lay with her father;
14　　　he did not know when she lay down or when she arose.
15　　　And on the next day, the first-born said to the younger,
16　　　'Behold, I lay last night with my father; let us make him
17　　　drink wine tonight also; then you go in and lie with him,
18　　　that we may preserve offspring through our father.' So
19　　　they made their father drink wine that night also; and the
20　　　younger arose, and lay with him; and he did not know
21　　　when she lay down nor when she arose." I didn't know. I
22　　　didn't know how else we could go on.
23　BABY: *(Simply, not sarcastically, a statement of fact)* You didn't
24　　　know. Before the first night you didn't know. But you
25　　　looked out the window. Remember? You told me that. You
26　　　looked out the window and you saw it raining. And then
27　　　you knew, Sissy, you knew the world wasn't over.
28　SISSY: Baby ... I'm sorry, Baby.
29　BABY: You sent me and I didn't have to go.
30　SISSY: I was so scared. I didn't want to be alone.
31　BABY: I know. We're sisters. I would have done it for you
32　　　anyway.

Vamp
by Ry Herman

Angela — 20s   Comic
Chloë — 20s

In this scene, the relationship between Chloë and Angela quickly develops from a casual conversation to a true bonding as the characters discover how much they have in common. The key to playing the repartee is for each actress to play the discoveries with energy and surprise, and to constantly find humor and fun in the other's company. The scene also leaves to the actresses' imagination just where the encounter takes place, and what properties might be helpful. For example, it could be a chance meeting at a swanky cocktail party, or on a park bench in New York or London, or in the laundromat one Saturday morning, etc. It may be performed sitting at a restaurant table or standing in line waiting for a bus or subway train. And the choice of environment can greatly affect the playing. No matter what choices are made, though, the audience should see by the end of the scene that the two women really do find joy and surprises in each other's company.

1   **ANGELA: Hey!**
2   **CHLOË:** *(Tentatively)* **Hey.**
3   **ANGELA: I ... uhh ... I met you a couple of months ago, at**
4   **Shelly's party ...? You were looking at the small bedroom ...**
5   **CHLOË: Oh! Right. You're Shelly's housemate, um —**
6   **ANGELA: Angela.**
7   **CHLOË: Right.**
8   **ANGELA: And you're ... Chloë?**
9   **CHLOË: Yeah.**
10 **ANGELA: You're the writer.**
11 **CHLOË: Well, I write.**
12 **ANGELA: That's so cool. I wish I was artistic.**

1   CHLOË: Well, I wouldn't — I mean, it's just what I do. And for
2   that matter, lately I haven't even been ... well, let's just say
3   I'm not exactly making a living at it.
4   ANGELA: But, that's kind of the point, isn't it? I don't mean the
5   whole "starving artist" thing, I just mean — it's not the
6   kind of thing you do just to make money, right?
7   CHLOË: I know I don't.
8   ANGELA: It's the kind of thing you have to be really passionate
9   about.
10 CHLOË: I think that's ... it's a little strong, don't you think?
11 ANGELA: OK, so why aren't you, I don't know, selling life
12   insurance? Making some money, investing in an IRA?
13 CHLOË: All right, yeah, I guess I am passionate about it.
14 ANGELA: I thought you might be. You've got the eyes.
15 CHLOË: Eyes?
16 ANGELA: Very intense eyes.
17 CHLOË: You're going to make me blush, here.
18 ANGELA: Ooooh, tempting. *(Pause.)* So, how do you survive if
19   writing doesn't pay?
20 CHLOË: I read bad plays.
21 ANGELA: Sorry?
22 CHLOË: I'm a slush pile reader for a publishing company. Our
23   nation's first line of defense against appalling theater.
24 ANGELA: Taking the bullets for the rest of us. How noble.
25 CHLOË: I'm not sure risking endless annoyance really counts
26   as a noble act.
27 ANGELA: Don't you ever get anything good?
28 CHLOË: Oh, yeah, of course. But they're no fun to talk about.
29   The fun ones are the ones which are really, really
30   astonishingly bad.
31 ANGELA: Like what?
32 CHLOË: Uhh ... like, *Where Did Grandma Go?* The only play I've
33   ever gotten written entirely in crayon.
34 ANGELA: You're kidding.
35 CHLOË: No.

1   ANGELA: By a kid?

2   CHLOË: No.

3   ANGELA: So where did Grandma go?

4   CHLOË: Grandma got spilled all over the carpet when little

5   Johnny knocked over the urn. The end. It was a children's

6   play, I think, but I've never been sure what the moral was

7   supposed to be.

8   ANGELA: Learn to use the vacuum cleaner?

9   CHLOË: Probably.

10 ANGELA: So, that's the worst play ever.

11 CHLOË: Oh, no. The grand prize winner has to be the Irish

12   Potato Famine musical.

13 ANGELA: Oh, my god.

14 CHLOË: The title was, *I'm Hungry.*

15 ANGELA: "I'm —" Wow.

16 CHLOË: It was ... remarkable.

17 ANGELA: I believe it. *(Pause.)*

18 CHLOË: Ummm ... I feel like I've been going on all about me.

19   What ... ummm ... what do you do for a living?

20 ANGELA: Me? I'm an astrophysicist.

21 CHLOË: A — wow. My turn to say "Wow."

22 ANGELA: Don't be silly.

23 CHLOË: No, I mean, that's impressive. That's not exactly

24   something you just fall into.

25 ANGELA: Well, I won't say getting my degree was easy or

26   anything ...

27 CHLOË: I would imagine not.

28 ANGELA: You know, everyone's always so surprised when I tell

29   them. I hate that. I mean, do I come across as dumb or

30   something?

31 CHLOË: No! No, not at all. It's more than that ... ummm ... well,

32   you ...

33 ANGELA: Don't look the part?

34 CHLOË: Don't fit the stereotype.

35 ANGELA: Oh, come on. You don't think I'm the type that likes

1   to stay up all night?

2   CHLOË: Fair enough. So is that your passion? Astrophysics?

3   ANGELA: Yes. Yes, it is. *(Pause.)* So, how come you didn't rent

4   the open room? We all thought you were great.

5   CHLOË: Entropy.

6   ANGELA: Entropy?

7   CHLOË: My cat. Shelly told me someone was really allergic to

8   cats, so I couldn't move in.

9   ANGELA: Oh. That was me. Sorry.

10   CHLOË: It's all right. I decided to stay where I was anyway. It's

11   ugly, but at least it's cheap.

12   ANGELA: I like your cat's name.

13   CHLOË: He is a living force of destruction and disorder. When

14   I first picked him up and was driving him home, my car

15   exploded.

16   ANGELA: Now you're making things up.

17   CHLOË: I wish I was. I can't afford to get another car.

18   ANGELA: But it wasn't — I mean, the cat didn't do anything to

19   make the car explode, right?

20   CHLOË: That's what I thought at first, too. That was before I

21   saw him run straight up a plaster wall and cling to the

22   ceiling. This is not a normal kitty.

23   ANGELA: You're an intriguing person.

24   CHLOË: Well, I have an intriguing cat.

Have Mercy
by Hope McIntyre

Nancy — 20s   Seriocomic
Sylvia — 20s

This scene has a powerful subtext for the actresses to play. Nancy is seven months pregnant and ashamed of herself because her own father committed incest with her and is the parent. She blames herself remorselessly despite Sylvia's efforts to change her opinion otherwise. The scene's structure needs to be carefully played because Nancy's guilt and hatred towards her parents and her baby, and Sylvia's own feelings of inadequacy, only gradually come to light. Nancy is unable to make any sense of her experience (except for her vague religious fears) because she's all alone now: her father has run off and her mother is in jail for murdering Nancy's other infants who were also the product of incest. Finally, the actresses will also notice a number of important discoveries here that both women make, and that change the tone of the scene at critical points. Despite the distance between Nancy and Sylvia at the beginning, both women change by the end and find some common ground between them as the scene concludes. See also a monolog from this play included in the section of monologs for women.

1 NANCY: Do ya want something? Some tea?
2 SYLVIA: Tea would be wonderful.
3 NANCY: *(Heaving herself out of the chair)* I don't know if we got
4   any cream, though.
5 SYLVIA: That's all right. On second thought, I'm fine.
6 NANCY: Ya sure?
7 SYLVIA: Yes. Please sit back down. You must find it pretty
8   taxing.
9 NANCY: What?
10 SYLVIA: Being in your condition? Especially in this heat?

1   NANCY: What do ya mean "my condition"?

2   SYLVIA: With child.

3   NANCY: Who says I am?

4   SYLVIA: I can tell —

5   NANCY: Did the doctor tell ya that? Did he go and tell everyone?

6   SYLVIA: I'm sorry, I didn't mean to upset you. It can't be easy.

7   NANCY: After the first time, it's never so bad.

8   SYLVIA: How many is this?

9   NANCY: I don't know. I don't keep track.

10 SYLVIA: And you've been feeling all right?

11 NANCY: Just fine.

12 SYLVIA: I don't mean to ask personal questions.

13 NANCY: I already had to talk to the J.P. to both the lawyers.

14   Gotta testify in the court, they says.

15 SYLVIA: I'm sure it can't be pleasant.

16 NANCY: What difference does it make? Everyone knows now.

17   Not much worse can happen.

18 SYLVIA: At least your father is gone. That must make things

19   better.

20 NANCY: Woulda been better if he'd-a gone without everyone

21   knowing. Now we gotta keep the farm running without

22   him, and we can't even sell the crop in town without

23   people whispering about the Robbins family disgrace.

24 SYLVIA: Their flapping tongues will quiet down with time.

25   *(Pause.)* You haven't asked about your mother? I've been

26   visiting her. *(No response.)* She is judging herself quite

27   harshly.

28 NANCY: It's getting time to milk the cows.

29 SYLVIA: I thought perhaps you could come with me the next

30   time I visit.

31 NANCY: I'm busy.

32 SYLVIA: Alright, let me help.

33 NANCY: Y'ever milked a cow?

34 SYLVIA: No.

35 NANCY: I didn't think so. Look, I just want all this done with.

1   SYLVIA: That's what we all want. We want your mother back
2   home so she can put all this behind her.
3   NANCY: Having her home won't do any good for us.
4   SYLVIA: What do you mean?
5   NANCY: Never mind.
6   SYLVIA: Don't you care what happens with your mother?
7   NANCY: About as much as she cared about what happened to
8   us.
9   SYLVIA: You don't mean that. I know you and your mother
10   were close.
11   NANCY: So were me and my father. But, I won't be paying much
12   mind to what happens to him.
13   SYLVIA: Your mother —
14   NANCY: Look, it don't matter what ya got to say! We're all
15   responsible. I coulda run. I tried, but I coulda tried
16   harder. Ma coulda done something. He did it. Ma let him.
17   We're all sinners and God will punish us. Instead of
18   repenting, Ma killed the babies. I don't know how. I never
19   seen her do it. But I'll tell ya that was no human child in
20   my belly. That was the devil. That was God's punishment.
21   And ya see, God's punishing me again. The whole town
22   knows it. I can never set foot in church again. I can never
23   get down on my knees in prayer again. God'd laugh at me.
24   *He* knows it's too late.
25   SYLVIA: God would not —
26   NANCY: In church once, the priest told the story about those
27   daughters. Those daughters who got their father drunk so
28   he'd make them have babies. I heard that story and I
29   thought real hard on it. I remember going to see the priest
30   after that service. And I asks him what about the father?
31   Shouldn't the father have known better and not done it?
32   No, he says, the father was under the power of the drink.
33   The father was seduced by his sinful daughters. Even
34   though the daughters was trying to give birth to children
35   for God, they were sinners and would only spawn the

1   **product of their sin. Well, in me right now is that product**
2   **of sin.**
3 **SYLVIA: Nancy, in you right now is a baby. Just a baby. A baby**
4   **that needs to be loved and cared for —**
5 **NANCY: I tell ya what. When this baby is born, you come round**
6   **here and I'll give it to ya. Then you can love it and care for**
7   **it all ya want.**
8 **SYLVIA: Nancy —**
9 **NANCY:** *(Calling Off)* **Jane! Jane, grab the bucket and let's get the**
10   **cows in.** *(She starts to exit.)* **Goodbye.**
11 **SYLVIA: I'm coming with you. It's time I learned how to milk a**
12   **cow.**
13 **NANCY: In those skirts?**
14 **SYLVIA: Why not?**
15 **NANCY: You ever tried to wash out cow shit? Ya best put some**
16   **boots on. There's extras inside the door.** *(NANCY exits.*
17   *SYLVIA looks down at her dress and pulls up her skirts to*
18   *tuck in.)*

Cell Cycle
by Cristina Pippa

Alicia — 19   Serious
Caitlyn — 16

The following scene occurs soon after the previous one from this same play included earlier in this section of scenes for two women. However, it comes immediately after the father's death, and now the roles of Alicia and Caitlyn are reversed. Caitlyn emerges here as the stronger of the two as she comforts Alicia; she also seems to have shed a lot of the sentimental religiosity that she professed in the earlier scene. What's particularly challenging here is that the scene calls for both actresses to express their characters' vulnerabilities authentically and with passionate sincerity. By the end of the scene, Alicia must discover a true need for her younger sister and perhaps even a reason to continue her career; while Caitlyn, too, must recognize the same sisterly bond and come to a new understanding of herself in the face of shared pain. Their embrace at the conclusion is the climactic point of the scene, and the actresses must carefully plot their development to that point.

1   **CAITLYN: He died, Alicia. After surgery, Dad ... passed on.**
2   **(*Pause.*) Do you want a hug or ... something? I wanted one.**
3   **When it happened there were all these people from Dad's**
4   **work and Pastor Owen wasn't there yet. I mean, when he**
5   **got there I felt so much better. But before I was looking**
6   **around and I was like ... wow ... we have no family. There's**
7   **no one here. And I know Dad told you to go and you**
8   **wanted to work, but I was kind of mad to be there by**
9   **myself. I was like ... why can't she do whatever she's doing**
10   **later? Why am I here by myself? I'm too young to watch my**
11   **Dad die by myself. So I'm sorry. I shouldn't have thought**
12   **that stuff. (*Pause.*) Ummmm ... you're still not saying**
13   **anything.**

1   ALICIA: I still can't believe he's dead. It's totally ... out of the
2   realm of possibility ... to me. Even though —
3   CAITLYN: I know.
4   ALICIA: I know it happened. I know you're standing there
5   telling me this, but you don't even look that sad. *(She*
6   *begins to cry.)*
7   CAITLYN: I am, really.
8   ALICIA: It's OK. You know what? I'm not that sad. About Dad, I
9   mean. I'm crying, but it's because I miss Mom. She was
10   everything. And now, I don't know.
11 CAITLYN: You can miss Mom, too.
12 ALICIA: I know I can. I do. I really ... hurt. But I can't miss him
13   because I don't feel like he's gone. I feel like he can't be
14   'cause he was always there. I can still see him ... and I can't
15   really see her. She's just more gone now.
16 CAITLYN: I hate to tell you this, Alicia, but he is gone. I was
17   there so I can tell you it.
18 ALICIA: I know.
19 CAITLYN: And you weren't there. And it wasn't beautiful at all.
20   His lips were cracked and his breath was making me feel
21   sick. His last breath. It was really loud and smelled
22   strange and I felt like I should kiss his cheek but I couldn't
23   'cause I was too creeped-out by my own dad. So no one
24   kissed his cheek. You would have. I know that. You
25   wouldn't have been scared.
26 ALICIA. I would. I'm scared now. I should be trying to make
27   you feel better but I have nothing.
28 CAITLYN: Pastor Owen did. Really. I'm OK. What he said
29   helped so much. And I don't know if you would like it, or
30   whatever.
31 ALICIA: You can tell me.
32 CAITLYN: He said Dad's body is just a ... I don't know ... a shell.
33   And his soul went to heaven, but little ... ummmm ... I
34   guess bits of it are still here, like attached to my soul and
35   attached to your soul. Mom's, too.

1 ALICIA: How do we know he went to heaven? If it's really his
2   fault that people died, that he didn't pay enough
3   attention, or respond —
4 CAITLYN: I don't believe it was his fault. I know he was human
5   but I guess it's like another sort of faith for me that he was
6   good. Maybe it's naïve.
7 ALICIA: It's not. Maybe I made Mom out to be too good. It just
8   means we loved them. And I don't know that anything was
9   his fault. I hope it wasn't.
10 CAITLYN: It was really hard for me to come here. I didn't know
11   where the room was. I had to ask, like, seven people. And
12   I saw that morgue you were talking about. It's really
13   creepy. Just to know it's there.
14 ALICIA: Thank you. For coming to tell me in person.
15 CAITLYN: I wish everything was the same as it used to be.
16 ALICIA: Like when?
17 CAITLYN: Like when we were kids. I miss being the four of us
18   in that house. How did you get over Mom dying?
19 ALICIA: How did you?
20 CAITLYN: I was young. I guess I am still.
21 ALICIA: I don't know that I did get over it. If I did, maybe
22   because we had Dad. And he had us. Remember how we
23   slept in their bed that night? You on one side of Dad and
24   me on the other. I was the only one who cried.
25 CAITLYN: That night.
26 ALICIA: I really believed in God then. I pictured Mom up in
27   heaven. Eating pizza, I think. Dad said to look up at the
28   stars and see her.
29 CAITLYN: To me, too. Yeah. This is much harder than I
30   imagined.
31 ALICIA: Yeah.
32 CAITLYN: You know, in half a second, there were all these
33   people from Dad's work. People I never met. I was like ...
34   supposed to put myself together.
35 ALICIA: I doubt anyone expected that.

1 CAITLYN: They kept asking what the rearrangements were
2   going to be.
3 ALICIA: Arrangements.
4 CAITLYN: What?
5 ALICIA: You said —
6 CAITLYN: I don't want to look at coffins.
7 ALICIA: I don't either.
8 CAITLYN: Pastor Owen's going to help.
9 ALICIA: I guess we should go.
10 CAITLYN: This place is so real-looking. I mean ... you know
11   what I mean? Like a mad scientist's laboratory in the
12   movies, except it's real.
13 ALICIA: I was so excited about working here. About finding
14   something. I don't even know what I was looking for. Or
15   why I thought I would find it.
16 CAITLYN: You have to come back here, OK?
17 ALICIA: Why?
18 CAITLYN: Dad was bragging to one of his war buddies when
19   you went to get dinner last night — about how you were
20   going to find the cure for cancer. So other people wouldn't
21   have to go through it. *(ALICIA gives CAITLYN a long hug.)*
22   He seems nice, Alicia.
23 ALICIA: Who?
24 CAITLYN: Your boyfriend.
25 ALICIA: Oh. Thanks.

Voices in My Head

by Ry Herman

Pat — Indeterminate age   Seriocomic

Sam — Indeterminate age

The following selection can be performed by any gender mix: two women or two men, or a man and a woman in either role. It appears in three sections of this book (scenes for two women, scenes for two men, and scenes for one man and one woman) to fully allow you to read it from all the possible perspectives. Although the scene is quickly read and seems brief, it offers actors plenty of opportunity to play the heartbeats in pauses and silences as Pat suspiciously "considers" the questions that Sam is asking, and Sam gradually discovers the true nature of their relationship. Additionally, the locale is undefined so the actors can explore what kind of environment would best support the action: outdoors on a park bench, in a living room, in an automobile, at the workplace, etc. Like the contentless scenes that are frequently used in acting classes, this scene allows actors to invent and improvise subtext, background and given circumstances, locale, movement, and gesture. The actors should also pay particular attention to the conclusion, deciding whether or not the philosophical impact of the final lines are really a show-stopping conclusion, or if there remains more to be said and done in a subsequent scene between the characters.

1   PAT: *(Appearing behind SAM)* **Hi.**

2   SAM: *(Startled)* **Pat! Hi.**

3   PAT: **Just came over to see how you were doing.**

4   SAM: **I'm not having a good day, Pat.**

5   PAT: **Sucks to be you.**

6   SAM: **Thanks. Thanks a lot.** *(Pause.)* **Say, Pat?**

7   PAT: **Yeah?**

8   SAM: **You know those voices I keep hearing?**

9   PAT: **Uh-huh?**

1   **SAM: They said something totally ludicrous. Want to hear it?**

2   **PAT: Sure.**

3   **SAM: They said you were trying to kill me.**

4   **PAT: Yep. That's pretty ridiculous.**

5   **SAM: Oh, yeah. I thought so.**

6   **PAT: I mean, what next?**

7   **SAM: Exactly. Next they'll be telling me, I don't know …**

8   **PAT: Your friends are imaginary and the voices are real?**

9   **SAM: Right, yeah.**

10   **PAT: You know, this is really a pretty weird conversation.**

11   **SAM: Ummm. Pat?**

12   **PAT: Yeah?**

13   **SAM: How did we meet?**

14   **PAT: Huh? I don't know. I think we were just hanging around**

15   **somewhere, or something. Something like that.**

16   **SAM: Something like that.**

17   **PAT: Yeah.** *(Pause.)* **What are you getting at here?**

18   **SAM: How come I've never seen you enter or leave a room?**

19   **PAT: What do you mean?**

20   **SAM: You just appear, or disappear, and I never see you do it.**

21   **PAT: What?**

22   **SAM: How about this. Walk through a door.**

23   **PAT: You're really getting freaky now.**

24   **SAM: Humor me. Make me feel better. Walk through a door.**

25   **PAT: I'm not going to encourage this.**

26   **SAM: Please.**

27   **PAT: No.**

28   **SAM: Walk through a door, Pat!** *(PAT draws a gun.)* **Or not. You**

29   **don't have to if you really don't want to. That's fine.**

30   **PAT: I didn't want to have to do this yet.**

31   **SAM: Pat, come on, put down the gun.**

32   **PAT: You shouldn't have forced my hand.**

33   **SAM: Why would you want to kill me? You're my best friend.**

34   **PAT: Haven't you figured it out yet? I'm not your best friend.**

35   **I'm not your friend at all.**

1   SAM: Who are you?
2   PAT: Oh, come on, think. You know me. You made me.
3   SAM: What are you talking about?
4   PAT: I'm all in your head. A projection. An alter ego. *(Pause.*
5   *SAM stares at PAT uncomprehendingly.)* **Multiple personality**
6   **disorder! Man, read a book.**
7   SAM: So why do you want to kill me?
8   PAT: I want your life. You're not using it anyway. So I figure it's
9   my turn.

Scenes for Two Men

Voices in My Head
by Ry Herman

Pat — Indeterminate age   **Seriocomic**
Sam — Indeterminate age

The following selection can be performed by any gender mix: two women or two men, or a man and a woman in either role. It appears in three sections of this book (scenes for two women, scenes for two men, and scenes for one man and one woman) to fully allow you to read it from all the possible perspectives. Although the scene is quickly read and seems brief, it offers actors plenty of opportunity to play the heartbeats in pauses and silences as Pat suspiciously "considers" the questions that Sam is asking, and Sam gradually discovers the true nature of their relationship. Additionally, the locale is undefined so the actors can explore what kind of environment would best support the action: outdoors on a park bench, in a living room, in an automobile, at the workplace, etc. Like the contentless scenes that are frequently used in acting classes, this scene allows actors to invent and improvise subtext, background and given circumstances, locale, movement, and gesture. The actors should also pay particular attention to the conclusion, deciding whether or not the philosophical impact of the final lines are really a show-stopping conclusion, or if there remains more to be said and done in a subsequent scene between the characters.

1 PAT: *(Appearing behind SAM)* **Hi.**
2 SAM: *(Startled)* **Pat! Hi.**
3 PAT: **Just came over to see how you were doing.**
4 SAM: **I'm not having a good day, Pat.**
5 PAT: **Sucks to be you.**
6 SAM: **Thanks. Thanks a lot.** *(Pause.)* **Say, Pat?**
7 PAT: **Yeah?**
8 SAM: **You know those voices I keep hearing?**
9 PAT: **Uh-huh?**

1   SAM: They said something totally ludicrous. Want to hear it?

2   PAT: Sure.

3   SAM: They said you were trying to kill me.

4   PAT: Yep. That's pretty ridiculous.

5   SAM: Oh, yeah. I thought so.

6   PAT: I mean, what next?

7   SAM: Exactly. Next they'll be telling me, I don't know ...

8   PAT: Your friends are imaginary and the voices are real?

9   SAM: Right, yeah.

10 PAT: You know, this is really a pretty weird conversation.

11 SAM: Ummm. Pat?

12 PAT: Yeah?

13 SAM: How did we meet?

14 PAT: Huh? I don't know. I think we were just hanging around

15   somewhere, or something. Something like that.

16 SAM: Something like that.

17 PAT: Yeah. *(Pause.)* What are you getting at here?

18 SAM: How come I've never seen you enter or leave a room?

19 PAT: What do you mean?

20 SAM: You just appear, or disappear, and I never see you do it.

21 PAT: What?

22 SAM: How about this. Walk through a door.

23 PAT: You're really getting freaky now.

24 SAM: Humor me. Make me feel better. Walk through a door.

25 PAT: I'm not going to encourage this.

26 SAM: Please.

27 PAT: No.

28 SAM: Walk through a door, Pat! *(PAT draws a gun.)* Or not. You

29   don't have to if you really don't want to. That's fine.

30 PAT: I didn't want to have to do this yet.

31 SAM: Pat, come on, put down the gun.

32 PAT: You shouldn't have forced my hand.

33 SAM: Why would you want to kill me? You're my best friend.

34 PAT: Haven't you figured it out yet? I'm not your best friend.

35   I'm not your friend at all.

1   SAM: Who are you?

2   PAT: Oh, come on, think. You know me. You made me.

3   SAM: What are you talking about?

4   PAT: I'm all in your head. A projection. An alter ego. *(Pause.*

5   *SAM stares at PAT uncomprehendingly.)* **Multiple personality**

6   **disorder! Man, read a book.**

7   SAM: So why do you want to kill me?

8   PAT: I want your life. You're not using it anyway. So I figure it's

9   my turn.

Portland
by Ruben Carbajal

Ed — 20s-30s   Comic
Cook — 20s-30s

This brief, snappy scene occurs in the kitchen of a restaurant where Ed has just landed a job, and the Cook must explain some of his duties to him. The rush hour background to the scene should lend a note of urgency, as Ed receives lessons on how to take orders and improve his self-image at the same time. The scene challenges actors by its brevity: though short, a lot of discoveries are made here by both characters. Actors should avoid rushing to the end of the short piece, and instead explore how physical actions and stage business can underscore the action of the scene, how comic actions deftly counterpoint the job orientation that Ed receives from Cook, and how each character clearly develops step-by-step in a definite way to end up in a very different place than where he began.

1 ED: Where are my eggs? Has anyone seen my eggs? There was a
2   side of bacon. Did anyone see my eggs? *(To himself)* Or the
3   pancakes. *(To others)* I had a plate of pancakes. Short
4   stack. Anyone?
5 COOK: What are you doing here, blocking everybody's way like
6   that?
7 ED: I have three orders that have completely disappeared. I'm
8   backed up nearly seven orders. The phone's ringing off
9   the hook.
10 COOK: Where are you putting your orders?
11 ED: On the carousel.
12 COOK: The carousel?
13 ED: Yes, on the carousel.
14 COOK: Well, that's your first mistake. No one back here pays any
15   mind to that thing. You have an order, you give it to me.

1 ED: Oh, I'm sorry. I didn't know.
2 COOK: What did you say?
3 ED: I said I was sorry.
4 COOK: Are you a sorry person?
5 ED: Well, no.
6 COOK: Then why do you say that you're sorry?
7 ED: It's just a manner of ...
8 COOK: You shouldn't denigrate yourself like that. Don't ever
9   say that you're sorry.
10 ED: I apologize then.
11 COOK: No. You don't apologize. *(Pause.)* Do you have any pride
12   in yourself?
13 ED: Sure, sure I do.
14 COOK: You don't seem to be someone who has much pride in
15   himself. That's the impression I get. I've seen you around
16   here, working. You don't give me that impression at all.
17   You should stop denigrating yourself. You understand?
18 ED: I guess.
19 COOK: You guess?
20 ED: No, I mean, I understand.

Deck the Stage
by Lindsay Price

Johan — Indeterminate age   **Comic**
Hans — Indeterminate age

This amusing scene depends as much upon the actors' intricate timing as it does on their skills in characterization. Despite the apparent similarity of the brothers — vocally and in physical actions — they are really very different. This is part of the comedy that the script brings out, and the scene thus challenges each actor to create a distinctively different personality for his competitive brother. It offers actors a wonderful range of unique choices to make. At the beginning of the scene, Johan and Hans come downstage. They match each other step for step, as if they don't want the other to get ahead.

1 JOHAN and HANS: Every year my brother and I ...
2 JOHAN: Partake in a competition ...
3 HANS: To choose the family Christmas tree.
4 JOHAN: It's been our job ...
5 JOHAN and HANS: Since we were seven years old.
6 HANS: We go with our Papa to the tree farm.
7 JOHAN: We each pick out a tree, and he chooses the winner.
8 HANS: It used to be ...
9 JOHAN and HANS: In the beginning ...
10 HANS: That we would decide on a tree together.
11 JOAN and HANS: But that was impossible. *(Each referring to the*
12   *other)* He's so competitive.
13 JOHAN: It's horrible.
14 JOHAN and HANS: He always has to have his way.
15 HANS: So now we get Papa to choose.
16 JOHAN: I have five wins and Hans only has four.
17 HANS: Johan always says he has five and I only have four.

1   JOHAN: He is such a sore loser.

2   HANS: The year that we were twelve I had double pneumonia

3   and Mama would not let me go to the tree farm, even

4   though I said I could go.

5   JOHAN: I picked the tree, Papa cut it down. It counts.

6   HANS: It does not count.

7   JOHAN: It counts!

8   JOHAN and HANS: He always gets like this. He always has to

9   have his way. He's impossible.

10 HANS: The morning of the trip is always bright and crisp and

11   clean.

12 JOHAN: I arise extra early to make sure I have all of my

13   equipment at hand.

14 HANS: Sturdy boots!

15 JOHAN: Strong gloves!

16 HANS: Binoculars for the scouting!

17 JOHAN: Tags to mark the trees.

18 JOHAN and HANS: One year, he tried to claim a tree that I had

19   clearly sighted first!

20 HANS: Now a tree cannot be claimed until it has a tag on it.

21 JOHAN: It's all his fault.

22 JOHAN and HANS: He's so competitive. *(They both take in a deep*

23   *breath.)*

24 JOHAN: We stand at the entrance to the tree farm ...

25 HANS: Breathing in the cool, crisp, morning air. *(They both*

26   *breathe in.)*

27 JOHAN and HANS: Our breath makes tiny clouds of mist which

28   fogs up our glasses. *(They both wipe their glasses.)*

29 JOHAN: Papa must set us off at exactly the same time.

30 JOHAN and HANS: *(Referring to each other)* He always tries to

31   cheat.

32 HANS: Johan's foot is over the line!

33 JOHAN: Hans's body is too far forward!

34 HANS: Inevitably Papa tells us to settle down or ...

35 JOHAN and HANS: He will pick the first scrawny broke bristle

1   spruce he can find and leave us for the dogs!

2 JOHAN: That Papa.

3 JOHAN and HANS: What a sense of humor. *(They both chuckle*

4   *for a moment. Then they both breathe in again.)*

5 JOHAN: We prepare.

6 HANS: We wait for the hand to go down.

7 JOHAN: The air is silent.

8 HANS: There is nothing but Papa's hand ...

9 JOHAN: And the trees.

10 JOHAN and HANS: *We're off!* *(The two start running in place.*

11   *They are frantically searching for the best tree.)*

12 JOHAN: Trees to the left!

13 HANS: Trees to the right!

14 JOHAN: Faster!

15 HANS: Faster!

16 JOHAN: Ah-ha!

17 HANS: Bah!

18 JOHAN: Too small!

19 HANS: Too tall!

20 JOHAN: Too fat!

21 HANS: Too puny!

22 JOHAN: Too old!

23 HANS: Too new!

24 JOHAN: Too much like the one we had last year.

25 JOHAN and HANS: I must find the perfect tree! I can't let him

26   beat me!

27 HANS: Beautiful pines.

28 JOHAN: Lush foliage.

29 HANS: Green as emeralds.

30 JOHAN: Ah-ha!

31 HANS: Ah-ha!

32 JOHAN: *Ah-ha!*

33 HANS: *Ah-ha!* *(They take a deep breath and jump up and down*

34   *for joy.)*

35 JOHAN and HANS: Every year it is so exhilarating! I can

1   **hardly wait!**

2 **JOHAN: And I know ...**

3 **HANS: Without a shadow of a doubt ...**

4 **JOHAN: That ...**

5 **HANS: The winner ...**

6 **JOHAN and HANS: Will be me!**

7 **HANS: Me.**

8 **JOHAN: Me.**

9 **HANS: Me!**

10 **JOHAN: *Me!***

11 **JOHAN and HANS: He is so impossible! He always has to have**

12   **his way!** *(The two cross their arms in frustration and stand*

13   *with their backs to each other.)*

The Poetry of Pizza
by Deborah Brevoort

Rebar — Indeterminate age   Comic
Soran — Indeterminate age

These two men are immigrants from Kurdistan who are living in Denmark, where Rebar owns a pizzeria. The scene challenges actors to develop in very different directions from beginning to end, and this is certainly part of the charming comedy expressed in their relationship. In the original play, a young American woman enters the pizzeria midway in the scene in order to take shelter in the doorway from a rainstorm outside. In this cutting, the actress doesn't appear on-stage but the two men can refer to her downstage at her entrance and exit. Only a dish towel and a pair of chairs or a bench are necessary for the scene, possibly with some music from a boom box played either On-stage or Off-stage.

1   REBAR: Soran ... you're playing that song again.
2   SORAN: Yes, Rebar.
3   REBAR: Soran ... are you crying?
4   SORAN: *(Trying to hide his face)* No!
5   REBAR: Soran ...
6   SORAN: *(Fighting back tears)* I no cry! I no cry!
7   REBAR: Look at you! You cry! It's that song. No more. You can
8   no more play that song! *(The song goes off.)*
9   SORAN: But I like! I like song!
10 REBAR: How can you like when it makes you cry? I cannot have
11   you like this in my pizzeria crying all the time!
12 SORAN: I no help it.
13 REBAR: Here. Wipe your eyes. *(REBAR hands him a kitchen*
14   *towel hanging from his back pocket.)*
15 SORAN: Thank you, my friend.
16 REBAR: What do you cry about today, my friend? Hmmm?

1   SORAN: Figs.

2   REBAR: Figs? *(SORAN shakes his head yes.)* **Yesterday you cry for**

3   **flowers, today you cry for the figs!**

4   SORAN: I miss my fig tree.

5   REBAR: OK. I go to bodega and buy you figs.

6   SORAN: I no like figs at bodega. Dry. No fresh.

7   REBAR: In Danmark, no fresh figs, Soran. You know this. Only

8   dry. No figs from Kurdistan. *(They both pronounce*

9   *Denmark "Dan-uh-mark.")*

10 SORAN: That's why I cry. For to ... for to ... taste the figs of

11   Kurdistan! *(He bursts into tears again.)* **To taste the figs**

12   **from my tree! The figs from my mother's tree!**

13 REBAR: Soran, my good man, you are homesick. That is all.

14   Here. Sit down. *(SORAN sits. REBAR sits next to him.)* **With**

15   **time, my friend, you will forget the taste of figs. Just like I**

16   **have forgotten.**

17 SORAN: No, no! Never! I will never forget the taste of the fig!

18 REBAR: Yes, you will.

19 SORAN: No! And I will never forget the pistachio!

20 REBAR: Oh! The pistachio!

21 SORAN: The taste of the pistachio!

22 REBAR: You are right! It is not possible to forget the taste of the

23   pistachio!

24 SORAN: I cry also for ... the pistachio!

25 REBAR: Stop! Stop! Or I will cry, too!

26 SORAN: I cry for ... to ... eat once again the pistachio of

27   Kurdistan! *(REBAR bursts into tears.)*

28 REBAR: Oh! Oh! To eat a pistachio!

29 SORAN: In Kurdistan, pistachio *soft* ...

30 REBAR: Oh!

31 SORAN: So soft, I open with my *tongue* ...

32 REBAR: Oh!

33 SORAN: But in Danmark ... Pistachio *hard*!

34 REBAR: *(Bitterly)* **Hard**, yes.

35 SORAN: So hard I open with *knife*!

1   REBAR: *(As if he's been stabbed)* **Ach!**

2   SORAN: *(With disdain)* **And in Danmark, pistachio *red*.** *(On*
3   *"red" both men stop crying and look at each other. Their*
4   *faces harden.)*

5   SORAN and REBAR: ***Red!*** *(In unison, they "spit" in disgust.)*

6   SORAN: **Pistachio no red, pistachio *green*!**

7   REBAR: **Green, *yes*!**

8   SORAN: **Why in Danmark pistachio *red*?** *(They sit quietly for a*
9   *moment unable to fathom this. SORAN hands REBAR his*
10   *dish towel.)*

11   SORAN: **I no like pistachio in Danmark. I no like Danmark.**

12   REBAR: *(Drying his eyes)* **Give it some time, my gentle friend.**
13   **You have only been here for two months.** *(They notice a*
14   *woman with an umbrella who enters the pizzeria.)*

15   SORAN: **Look, Rebar! A flower has come to pizzeria.**

16   REBAR: **No, Soran, that is not a flower, that is an *umbrella*. You**
17   **have to work harder at your English, my friend. You**
18   **always get the words wrong.**

19   SORAN: **No! I know what I say. I know umbrella. But Rebar, I do**
20   **not look with my eyes only, I look also with my heart. And**
21   **with *heart* I see *flower*!** *(SORAN is thunderstruck.)* **I see ...**
22   ***beautiful* flower ... !**

23   REBAR: **I see *American* flower.**

24   SORAN: **American? How you know?**

25   REBAR: **The shoes.** *(SORAN is mesmerized.)* **Soran! What are**
26   **you doing!**

27   SORAN: **I make for her pizza. I make for her ... *beautiful* pizza.**

28   REBAR: **No, Soran, no pizza for American flower. American**
29   **flowers are no good.**

30   SORAN: **Why no good?**

31   REBAR: **They are "easy to pick."**

32   SORAN: **How you mean?** *(REBAR makes a lewd gesture.)* **No!**

33   REBAR: **Yes! And American flowers have disease!**

34   SORAN: **Disease?**

35   REBAR: **From the *sex*!**

1 SORAN: *(Watching the young woman)* **She no have disease!**
2 **REBAR: Oh, yes!**
3 **SORAN: How you know?**
4 **REBAR: Look how she stands in the door**
5 **SORAN: She look beautiful standing in door!**
6 **REBAR: No, Soran. She looks no good in the door like that.** *(The*
7 *young woman moves away from the doorway.)*
8 **SORAN: Oh, no! She go! The flower go!** *(SORAN starts to run*
9 *after her.)* **Wait!**
10 **REBAR: Soran! Where are you going?**
11 **SORAN: Wait! Please!**
12 **REBAR: Soran ...**
13 **SORAN:** *(Looking after her)* **I love her.**
14 **REBAR: What?**
15 **SORAN: I love American flower.**
16 **REBAR. No. You. Don't.**

Scenes for One Man and One Woman

V-E Day
by Faye Sholiton

Bernie — 23   **Romantic**
Evie — 19

This play is set both in the present and during WWII, when "the greatest generation" pulled together as a nation to fight the Axis powers overseas and on the home front. Evelyn is recalling her youthful days as the editor of a hometown newsletter that she published for the troops, and especially the day when she received a marriage proposal from her beau, Bernie. In the original play, this scene is a nostalgic flashback where the older Evelyn regrets her missed opportunities, since at the time she rejected Bernie's proposal. Actors will find the scene structure fun to play — particularly the surprises and discoveries as well as the moments following Bernie's proposal. The piece also offers opportunities for a certain amount of research into the historical period, especially the way in which women's roles were changing as they took up traditional male occupations on the home front. But the most challenging aspects of the scene are the mixed characterizations, in the sense that both Evie and Bernie emerge neither as wholly good and virtuous nor wholly selfish and shortsighted. See also another scene from this play included in this section of scenes for one man and one woman.

1 EVIE: Your gals are at full employment, all helping in the
2   effort. You can't walk off a job now, even if you want to.
3   Shortages are mounting, of course. Serving butter is a
4   thing of the past. The bootleggers don't know whether to
5   bootleg rye whiskey or rye bread. But there's a good
6   feeling in the air, as everyone pulls together. The new
7   overworked saying is "for the duration."
8 BERNIE: Ho, ho, ho? *(EVIE looks up, screams, and runs to the*
9   *door for BERNIE. He wears a Santa beard and a carnation*

1   *and carries a duffel bag.)*

2   **EVIE: Bernie? Oh, my god! Tell me it's really you!**

3   **BERNIE: I saw the old Nash, in the drive. I thought my heart**

4   **was gonna pop right out of my chest!**

5   **EVIE: Ya might've warned me, ya big lug!**

6   **BERNIE: I was hoping for something a little warmer.** *(EVIE and*

7   *BERNIE embrace.)* **Jesus, let me look at you ...**

8   **EVIE: I'm gonna kill that sister of yours. She never said a word!**

9   **BERNIE: They don't know, either. I came straight here.**

10 **EVIE: From New Mexico?**

11 **BERNIE: Three days. Four trains. Talk about a sight for sore**

12   **eyes!**

13 **EVIE: What can I get you? Let me put up coffee ...**

14 **BERNIE: How 'bout something stronger? For courage.** *(He*

15   *kisses her again. She pours him bourbon that he devours.)*

16 **EVIE: You want some Coke with that?**

17 **BERNIE: Look, honey. I gotta tell ya something.**

18 **EVIE: Me, first!**

19 **BERNIE: It's pretty important ...**

20 **EVIE: No-no. Close your eyes!** *(EVIE gathers several papers.)*

21 **BERNIE: Now?**

22 **EVIE: Hold your horses!**

23 **BERNIE: I only got a week ...** *(EVIE displays several newspaper*

24   *clippings.)*

25 **EVIE: OK ... Now. Voila!**

26 **BERNIE: Very impressive.**

27 **EVIE: Read the credits!**

28 **BERNIE: These are swell. Really swell.**

29 **EVIE: This one was from Flag Day, at the Art Museum. They**

30   **turned the grounds into a huge Victory Garden. The kids**

31   **were collecting cans. If you look, you can see the stars and**

32   **stripes reflected in the can ...**

33 **BERNIE: Wow.**

34 **EVIE: Which one?**

35 **BERNIE: "Three AM, Statler Bar." Who's the couple?**

1   **EVIE: I don't know. I just kind of *caught* them. He was shipping**
2   **out the next day.**
3   **BERNIE: It's like they were the two last people in the world.**
4   **EVIE: Exactly! Your hands are shaking!**
5   **BERNIE: All right. My turn?** *(BERNIE pulls an invisible ring from*
6   *his pocket and takes EVIE's left hand.)*
7   **EVIE: Is this some kind of joke?**
8   **BERNIE: I just made up my mind, on the train from St. Louis to**
9   **Chicago! But go find a jeweler open on Christmas.** *(Pause.)*
10   **Here. Try it on. This was the best I could do.** *(He places the*
11   *invisible ring on EVIE's finger.)* **I'm afraid I didn't have a lot**
12   **of time.**
13   **EVIE: Apparently not!**
14   **BERNIE: I'm heading overseas, any day now. And every night, I**
15   **wake up in a cold sweat, thinking I'm gonna read about**
16   **you and somebody else in *Keeping Posted*. You're always**
17   **writing about the canteens, and all the fellas you're**
18   **hauling around in that ambulance ... Do you understand**
19   **that I'm more afraid of losing you than ... anything?**
20   **EVIE: I'll put up that coffee.**
21   **BERNIE: Please, sweetheart, don't make this any more difficult**
22   **...** *(BERNIE gets down on one knee.)* **Will you be my lawful**
23   **wedded?**
24   **EVIE: Oh, Bernie ... You know I ... When?**
25   **BERNIE: Sunday.**
26   **EVIE: *This* Sunday?**
27   **BERNIE: Why, you had other plans?**
28   **EVIE: For one thing, it's nearly the end of the month and I have**
29   **an issue to get out! And besides, I promised Pop this**
30   **weekend at the hospital ... They're short staffed, on**
31   **account of the holidays.**
32   **BERNIE: I see.**
33   **EVIE: Don't get me wrong, darling. But I need time. You know I**
34   **need time!** *(Pause.)* **You're not angry with me ... Look, I'm**
35   **wearing your ring. Doesn't that tell you something?**

1   **BERNIE:** It's thirty carats. I wanted more.

2   **EVIE:** Thirty's fine.

3   **BERNIE:** Honest?

4   **EVIE:** I'll have to have it sized, of course. And insured. *(They*

5   *kiss.)* **Overseas, huh.**

6   **BERNIE:** So it's official, right?

7   **EVIE:** But let's keep it *entre nous*, for the time being.

8   **BERNIE:** Tell you what. When you're ready to give the "all

9   clear," just put it in Lil's Column. And then the whole

10   world will know ...

11   **EVIE:** You bet.

12   **BERNIE:** Say! How 'bout we celebrate tonight, at the Terrace

13   Room? They don't do the Jersey Bounce where I'll be

14   going.

15   **EVIE:** Meantime, go home and see your folks. *(Pause.)* **What.**

16   **BERNIE:** I could use a lift. *(EVIE tosses him some keys.)*

17   **EVIE:** Still remember how to start 'er up?

18   **BERNIE:** Single engine, right?

19   **EVIE:** I'll be there in two shakes. *(EVIE waits a beat, then*

20   *removes the invisible ring and puts it in a dining room*

21   *drawer.)*

Geography
by Shirley King

Hannah — 20s   Seriocomic
Albert — 20s

In the fall of 2005, the Gulf coast of the United States was struck by a horrific hurricane. The storm destroyed all public services in the region, devastated thousands of buildings, destroyed the city of New Orleans, killed thousands, and displaced hundreds of thousands of people who were temporarily relocated to shelters. The following scene takes place in Lakeland, Mississippi, one of many small towns where thousands lined up daily for food, gasoline, and other supplies. Hannah and Albert, two complete strangers, are temporarily thrown together in this chaos, and Albert has just invited her to share a ride with him to Galveston. During the course of the scene, they begin to feel each other out, eventually discovering more surprises about each other than either had expected. The scene develops through a series of climaxes that must be carefully structured. The actors should also pay attention to the many discoveries and realizations that punctuate the scene, controlling the climaxes and leading to a recognition of Albert and Hannah's core values at the every end.

1 **HANNAH: How long do we have to wait?**
2 **ALBERT: 'Til I fill this gas can. Quit whinin'. The National**
3   **Guard set this up and all the gas is free. There's people**
4   **ahead of us.**
5 **HANNAH: Duh.**
6 **ALBERT: I said you could ride to Galveston with me, but you**
7   **gotta stop bein' so negative.**
8 **HANNAH: OK, we leave California for hooterville, then my**
9   **auntie dies and leaves us her house, then like, poof! The**
10   **house is gone and so is my mom —**
11 **ALBERT: That's my fault?**

1   HANNAH: — and now I'm with a guy who passes out all the time —

2   ALBERT: I never pass out when I drive.

3   HANNAH: — and if we ever get to Galveston I still have to hitch

4   to Houston, so yeah, I should be really up about all this.

5   Look, my mom's the positive one and I'm not. That way we

6   balance each other out.

7   ALBERT: You know, our house is gone, too. You don't hear me

8   fussin'.

9   HANNAH: You know your parents are alive.

10 ALBERT: My dad's got lung problems and can't work. My mom

11   sews and cleans for people. The house was all they had.

12 HANNAH: OK, I guess things aren't so good for you either.

13 ALBERT: Duh.

14 HANNAH: Why isn't this line moving?

15 ALBERT: I dunno.

16 HANNAH: I'm gonna run up there and ask. *(HANNAH tries to*

17   *grab the gas can, but ALBERT won't let her.)*

18 ALBERT: No. That's not how we do things here. This isn't

19   California, you know, where people get what they want all

20   the time.

21 HANNAH: Obviously you've never been to California.

22 ALBERT: Never been and no desire to go.

23 HANNAH: Right. Because this is such a great place to live. Some

24   people might say, hey, you know, since my house keeps

25   getting totaled maybe I might think about living

26   somewhere else. How come this line's not moving? The

27   fumes are making me sick. Doesn't it ever cool off here?

28 ALBERT: We're all leavin', OK? We gotta leave. No food, no place

29   to stay, but I'm comin' back quick as I can. I was born in

30   Lakeland.

31 HANNAH: Well, I was born in Turlock, but that doesn't mean —

32 ALBERT: Could you just shut up for a while?

33 HANNAH: So how come you do wrestling? What's with that?

34 ALBERT: You ever slam anyone to the mat?

35 HANNAH: No, but I'd like to.

1   ALBERT: OK, so that's what I get to do and nobody puts me in
2   jail. I might be able to make a living at it.
3   HANNAH: But that stuff's all fake.
4   ALBERT: Entertainment. Like the movies. Pro wrestlers,
5   they're just puttin' on a good show.
6   HANNAH: OK, you fake killing each other and everyone knows
7   it's fake but they pay to see it anyway. Got it. You know,
8   that's really bizarre. So what do you do for fun? Skin
9   rattlesnakes? Hunt possum?
10 ALBERT: You want to go to Galveston or not?
11 HANNAH: Not really. Maybe we could go to Houston instead.
12 ALBERT: Maybe you could just shut up. You don't even know
13   what Galveston's like.
14 HANNAH: Galveston: located in Galveston County on the east
15   Texas coast. Named after Bernardo de Gálves,
16   incorporated by Congress in 1839. Worst natural disaster
17   in U.S. history was caused by a hurricane that hit
18   Galveston in 1900. Over eight thousand people died. You
19   sure you want to go there? Houston's much safer.
20 ALBERT: So you know all that geography. So what? Mud devils?
21   They look like giant salamanders. In Missouri they call
22   'em hellbenders. Gets hot there, too. Hotter'n hell there in
23   the summer.
24 HANNAH: What?
25 ALBERT: Mud devils. You asked last night, remember? I know
26   stuff, too.
27 HANNAH: Are you punkin' me about the mud devils?
28 ALBERT: Maybe.
29 VOICE: *(From Off-stage)* Lakeland is damaged beyond repair. No
30   buildings survived and our sources report at least fifty
31   people dead. And this is not the final body count. The
32   National Weather Service predicted this hurricane, but
33   nobody listened.
34 ALBERT: I don't care about anyone's sources. We're gonna
35   rebuild and they can't stop us.

1 HANNAH: Omigod. Fifty people in this town died? Look, maybe
2   I act mean, but I'm actually trying to be hopeful.
3 ALBERT: Don't seem like it.
4 HANNAH: This morning I think I saw God — maybe I just have
5   a fever. But what she said was I needed to —
6 ALBERT: God's not a woman. Don't you read the Bible?
7 HANNAH: Why can't God be a woman?
8 ALBERT: One thing I know, God has a plan for us. That's why
9   he spared some folks. I volunteered for Search and Rescue
10   but they said I wasn't trained. I'm thinkin' they don't want
11   me findin' bodies of people I know.
12 HANNAH: I keep wondering, did God actually have a plan for
13   all those people who didn't make it?
14 ALBERT: He called 'em home to heaven.
15 HANNAH: All of them? What about the sinners?
16 ALBERT: You know, that's a stupid-ass question.
17 HANNAH: I'm, like, really stressed — you know? OK, here's the
18   deal: you don't get in my face, I don't get in yours. We
19   could try that.
20 ALBERT: How about you stop tryin' to be so cute?
21 HANNAH: You call this cute? Hey, the line's actually moving.
22   How can that be?
23 ALBERT: I keep wonderin', when's the President gonna get
24   here? We'all voted for him.
25 HANNAH: We'all didn't.
26 ALBERT: Well, you shoulda. He took action when the terrorists
27   struck, got the troops mobilized to go over there and hunt
28   down WMDs, put a dictator in jail. He's a righteous man.
29 HANNAH: Oh, wow. OK, I'm not going there right now but one
30   thing I know for sure, this country's in, like, major trouble
31   and the hurricane didn't help.
32 ALBERT: That's crap. We're re-buildin' here and so is New
33   Orleans, and we'll go on just like we always do. The
34   government's gonna help us. OK?
35 VOICE: *(From Off-stage)* Today House Speaker Dennis Hastert

1   said this of federal assistance for hurricane-devastated
2   New Orleans: "It makes no sense to spend billions of
3   dollars to rebuild a city that's seven feet under sea level."

BFE
by Julia Cho

Panny – 14   **Comic**
Hugo – 20

Panny is a young student trying to discover herself while attending middle school. Although Julia Cho's play is set in Arizona, where this conflicted Asian-American girl is growing up, the play's title refers to "the middle of nowhere" and can stand for any small town or suburban wasteland. Hugo is a friend of Panny's schoolmate, and Panny has called him by accident one night. The scene poses an interesting challenge to the actors who must create a compelling relationship only by means of their telephone conversation, in two separate spaces on-stage – a relationship that begins to take both of them on a journey to somewhere they've never been. Although the encounter seems very natural and real, actors should pay special attention to the scene's structure. They should fully experience the breaks in the action at the beginning, where the two call each other back and where Panny speaks directly to the audience. Also note the scene's accelerating tempo, and the way the author gradually introduces humorous elements later on. Although the scene was originally divided into two sections (as time passes), the entire piece can effectively be played as a single scene. In the original production, Hugo played the scene drinking from an orange juice carton, while Penny just lay on her bed idly staring at the ceiling. But there are numerous other choices for physical actions that the actors can make in order to shape the physical circumstances. At the start of the scene, Hugo's phone rings.

1   **HUGO: Hello?**
2   **PANNY: Hi, is Nancy there?**
3   **HUGO: Who's Nancy?**
4   **PANNY: Her mom gave me this number?**
5   **HUGO:** *(Mimicking her intonation)* **Why do you make a**
6   **statement as if it's a question?**

1   PANNY: You're making fun of me?
2   HUGO: Oh, come on? Have a sense of − ? *(She hangs up.)* OK,
3   don't. *(PANNY calls again.)* Hello?
4   PANNY: Oh, shoot.
5   HUGO: You know, dialing's not that hard.
6   PANNY: Why are you so obnoxious?
7   HUGO: *Moi? (PANNY hangs up again. HUGO dials. PANNY's*
8   *phone rings.)*
9   PANNY: Hello?
10 HUGO: I am not obnoxious.
11 PANNY: How'd you do that?
12 HUGO: I'm psychic. It's called Caller ID. Hmmmm. There's no
13   description. You sound cute. Are you? *(PANNY hangs up.*
14   *HUGO dials. The phone rings. PANNY hesitantly picks it up.)*
15   Don't hang up.
16 PANNY: I'm sorry, I think you have the wrong number −
17 HUGO: I have a question for you.
18 PANNY. Listen. I don't know who you're −
19 HUGO: Question. Would you rather have dark, curly hair all
20   over your body *or* would you rather have a small, curly tail
21   that no one can see? Hello? Not good, huh? OK, how about:
22   Would you rather sneeze cottage cheese or cry vegetable
23   oil? You're being quiet. Does this mean you're not going to
24   hang up? I am very bored. If you do not talk to me I will be
25   forced to watch some rather unpalatable television. OK,
26   easier question. Would you rather talk to me on the phone
27   or would you rather I hang up? *(Pause.)*
28 PANNY: I would rather ... talk on the phone.
29 HUGO: Well, peachy. So would I.
30 PANNY: *(To audience)* And that's how I met Hugo.
31
32 *(Time has passed. PANNY and HUGO are on the phone. HUGO's*
33   *reading out of a huge textbook.)*
34 HUGO: This is my favorite: trichotillomania. That's when you
35   obsessively pluck hair from your head and then you eat it.

1   PANNY: Gross.

2   HUGO: I love this stuff.

3   PANNY: This is homework?

4   HUGO: For Psych class.

5   PANNY: Psych? What kind of class is that?

6   HUGO: I don't know ... a social science class?

7   PANNY: ... Where do you go to school?

8   HUGO: Southwest Community.

9   PANNY: That's college.

10 HUGO: Duh.

11 PANNY: How old are you?

12 HUGO: Twenty. Took some time off after high school, so I

13   started late. How about you?

14 PANNY: I'm ... eighteen.

15 HUGO: Where d'you go?

16 PANNY: Brimsdale. High School.

17 HUGO: No kidding. I went to O'Connor. You figure out what

18   you're going to do after you graduate?

19 PANNY: I don't know, move?

20 HUGO: Why? It's so beautiful here.

21 PANNY: Are you kidding me?

22 HUGO: You don't think so?

23 PANNY: No.

24 HUGO: Come on, the sunsets? The mountains?

25 PANNY: I guess.

26 HUGO: You should take some time and really look at it, Panny.

27   It's like that French saying, "*Si vous prenez mes yeux,*

28   *vous les trouverez beaux.*"

29 PANNY: Wow.

30 HUGO: Means, "If you look into my eyes, you will find them

31   beautiful."

32 PANNY: Where'd you learn French like that? In France?

33 HUGO: No ... in French class.

34 PANNY: Right. So what did you do after you graduated?

35 HUGO: I went on my mission.

1   PANNY: Your what?

2   HUGO: My mission.

3   PANNY: Like a superhero?

4   HUGO: No. Like a Mormon.

5   PANNY: You're a Mormon?

6   HUGO: Why do you say it like that?

7   PANNY: 'Cause you seem kind of normal is all.

8   HUGO: Gee. Thanks.

9   PANNY: No, I just meant. Mormon. So then you can't swear or

10   anything.

11   HUGO: Nope.

12   PANNY: So what do you do when you get really mad?

13   HUGO: I don't know. I don't remember the last time I got mad.

14   PANNY: Really?

15   HUGO: Stuff just doesn't bother me.

16   PANNY: Because of your religion?

17   HUGO: No, because of my personality.

18   PANNY: So where did they send you? For your mission? Like

19   deepest Africa?

20   HUGO: No. Baltimore.

21   PANNY: What kind of missionary goes to Baltimore?

22   HUGO: Hey, people in Baltimore are just as needy.

23   PANNY: For what? Polygamy?

24   HUGO: Panny, we don't do that anymore.

25   PANNY: No?

26   HUGO: No, the crazy ones out in the sticks, the fundamentalists,

27   they do it.

28   PANNY: Oh, so the normal Mormons, you guys just own Pepsi.

29   HUGO: Ha-ha.

30   PANNY: So your father has only one wife? You didn't grow up in

31   a compound?

32   HUGO: No. Anyway, my dad's dead.

33   PANNY: Oh. God. I'm sorry.

34   HUGO: Don't be. Happened a long time ago.

35   PANNY: I don't really have a father either.

1   HUGO: Did he – ?

2   PANNY: No, he's alive. At least, I think he is. He and my mom

3   never got married. She got pregnant with me by accident.

4   He took off.

5   HUGO: He couldn't handle it?

6   PANNY: I don't know. No one ever says. *(Pause.)*

7   HUGO: Hey. Tell me something you've never told anyone

8   before.

9   PANNY: What?

10   HUGO: Tell me something you've never told anyone else before.

11   PANNY: Why?

12   HUGO: Because I want to hear it.

13   PANNY: OK ... I ... like what kind of thing?

14   HUGO: Any kind of thing.

15   PANNY: OK. Um. There was this one time. I was sitting here, at

16   my desk. It was really late and I only had my desk lamp on.

17   I was stretching or something and happened to catch my

18   reflection in the window. And I don't know – the quality

19   of the light or something – but it was like for this really

20   brief moment, I wasn't me. I actually seemed ... beautiful.

21   I'm only saying that because, see, in reality, I'm not. I'm

22   not beautiful. At all. But it was like because it was so late

23   and there was absolutely no one around, I was beautiful –

24   a little. And I thought, oh, it's like my beautiful self is this

25   imaginary friend, my inner Snuffalupagus, that only I can

26   see. I don't know. That was stupid. You tell me something,

27   OK? Something you've never said to anyone.

28   HUGO: There's nothing. I've said everything.

29   PANNY: No secrets?

30   HUGO: None.

31   PANNY: Come on.

32   HUGO: Something I've never said to anyone ... OK. I've never

33   liked anyone's voice half as much as I like yours.

34   PANNY: Really?

35   HUGO: Really.

Falling
by William Borden

Reina – 20s   **Serious**
Zaki – 20s

The following selection is actually a complete ten-minute play, but it functions equally well as a scene exercise in acting classes. The action takes place in the air, on September 11, 2001, when Zaki and Reina jump from the World Trade Center in New York. It permits a variety of choices for staging, including that of the author's: "Side by side Reina and Zaki face the audience, they show no fear or panic, everything is understated." Structurally, the scene has a very clear and powerful development towards the point where the couple falls in love close to the end; so it offers the actors many opportunities to explore their all-too-brief relationship and the growth of their feelings, discoveries, and conclusions. Actors would be well-advised to closely study the playwright's stage directions while rehearsing the piece, because the pauses and gestures are very helpful and expressive.

1   **REINA: Jump?** *(ZAKI doesn't answer.)* **Jump?**

2   **ZAKI: Jump?**

3   **REINA: Jump.**

4   **ZAKI: Jump.**

5   **REINA: Hold my hand.** *(He takes her hand.)*

6   **ZAKI: Now?**

7   **REINA: Now?**

8   **ZAKI: Now.** *(They take a step forward.)*

9   **REINA: How long will it take?**

10   **ZAKI: Not long.**

11   **REINA: We're high.**

12   **ZAKI: Gravity.**

13   **REINA: Gravity.**

14   **ZAKI: Thirty-two feet per second per second.**

1 **REINA: Galileo?**

2 **ZAKI: High school physics.**

3 **REINA: How long?**

4 **ZAKI: Not long.**

5 **REINA: They say time slows down.**

6 **ZAKI: It's the mind.**

7 **REINA: Giving us more time?**

8 **ZAKI: Giving us more time.**

9 **REINA: I want to get it over with.**

10 **ZAKI: I want as much time as possible.**

11 **REINA: How much time?**

12 **ZAKI: Over a hundred floors —**

13 **REINA: A hundred and seven.**

14 **ZAKI: A hundred and seven floors ... thirteen hundred feet ...**

15 *(He lets go of her hand to feel in his pockets.)* **I must have left**

16 **my calculator.** *(He calculates in his head.)* **Ten seconds.** *(She*

17 *takes his hand.)*

18 **REINA: That's not long.**

19 **ZAKI: It'll seem long.**

20 **REINA: It feels slow.**

21 **ZAKI: It's our minds. Giving us more time.**

22 **REINA: It's my first day at this job.**

23 **ZAKI: It's my last.**

24 **REINA: Yes. My last day, too.**

25 **ZAKI: No, really my last. I got a new job. I start tomorrow. Better**

26 **salary, more responsibility.**

27 **REINA: Different building?**

28 **ZAKI: Different building.**

29 **REINA: That's good.** *(Pause.)* **I don't think I turned the lights out**

30 **in my apartment.**

31 **ZAKI: I was supposed to call my mother this morning.**

32 **REINA: Loose ends.**

33 **ZAKI: You think, there's always tomorrow.**

34 **REINA: It's taking a long time.**

35 **ZAKI: It only seems that way.**

1   REINA: Gravity.

2   ZAKI: We're accelerating. The acceleration of gravity.

3   REINA: Time seems to get slower and slower.

4   ZAKI: Every instant we're falling faster.

5   REINA: So slow.

6   ZAKI: It's the mind.

7   REINA: It must be the mind.

8   ZAKI: The mind does strange things.

9   REINA: The mind is a beautiful thing.

10 ZAKI: Yes.

11 REINA: Life.

12 ZAKI: Beautiful.

13 REINA: Short.

14 ZAKI: Too short.

15 REINA: Bad luck.

16 ZAKI: Meant to be.

17 REINA: God's plan?

18 ZAKI: What else?

19 REINA: Bad luck.

20 ZAKI: Fate.

21 REINA: Destiny?

22 ZAKI: We can't know everything.

23 REINA: Bad bad luck.

24 ZAKI: I'm Zaki.

25 REINA: I'm Reina. Reina Steinberg.

26 ZAKI: Zaki Farqez. Born in New Jersey.

27 REINA: Brooklyn. Will it hurt?

28 ZAKI: No.

29 REINA: I think it will hurt.

30 ZAKI: Over in an instant.

31 REINA: If we had met sooner.

32 ZAKI: I wish we had.

33 REINA: Who knows —?

34 ZAKI: You and me —

35 REINA: A Jew —

1   ZAKI: A Muslim –

2   REINA: Who knows?

3   ZAKI: Love.

4   REINA: Children.

5   ZAKI: Long happy lives.

6   REINA: True love.

7   ZAKI: Might have been.

8   REINA: People can fall in love –

9   ZAKI: In ten seconds.

10   REINA: Time slows down.

11   ZAKI: You never have enough time.

12   REINA: A hundred years isn't enough time.

13   ZAKI: Life is short.

14   REINA: Time flies.

15   ZAKI: A lifetime can seem like an instant.

16   REINA: Ten seconds –

17   ZAKI: A lifetime.

18   REINA: Maybe even one second of love lasts, somehow,

19   somewhere, forever. Maybe love is a plunge into eternity.

20   ZAKI: Maybe all we have is this moment.

21   REINA: Maybe that's all anyone ever has, this moment.

22   ZAKI: Every moment –

23   REINA: Every second –

24   ZAKI: – a sliver –

25   REINA: – of eternity.

26   ZAKI: We're flying, Reina.

27   REINA: We're flying into love.

28   ZAKI: Eternity.

29   REINA: Love.

30   ZAKI: Love.

31   *(Blackout.)*

32   A VOICE: The fall lasted ten seconds. They struck the ground at

33   just less than one hundred fifty miles per hour – not fast

34   enough to cause unconsciousness while falling ... They

35   jumped alone, in pairs, and in groups. (*U.S.A. Today*)

Shot At
by Adam J. Ruben

Jason – 20s   **Romantic**
Kendra – 20s

The following selection is actually a complete ten-minute play, but it functions equally well as a scene exercise in advanced acting classes. Actors should explore the comic timing of the dialog in different sections of the scene: does it develop like fast-paced repartee? Is it fragmented and breathless? Where does it become slow-moving and hesitant as they explore each other's feelings? Are the indicated pauses short or long? The scene also challenges actors to explore and play a consistent line of development from beginning to end: how much of Kendra's behavior, for example, is sincere and caring, and how much of it is designed to manipulate Jason into staying the night? Is Jason's struggle to overcome his fear and trembling greater than his struggle to admit to himself how attractive Kendra really is? Obviously both characters end up feeling differently at the end of the scene than they did at the beginning — what discoveries, confessions, conclusions, or decisions do they make during the scene in order to develop in this way?

1   (*The scene is Kendra's apartment. The entrance is on one
2   side, the doorway to her bedroom on the other side, and
3   Upstage is a window with a chest of drawers, atop which sits
4   a large potted plant. Kendra has been crying as the scene
5   begins. There is an urgent knocking at her door which she
6   ignores. The knock comes again.*)
7   **JASON:** *(From Off-stage)* **Kendra!**
8   **KENDRA: Go away.**
9   **JASON:** *(From Off-stage)* **It's an emergency! You have to let me
10   in!** (*JASON pounds on the door again.*)
11   **KENDRA: You left, remember? Leave me alone.**
12   **JASON:** *(Off-stage, desperately)* **Kendra, please! It's not about us!**

1   *(She crosses to the door and waits there.)* **C'mon, please?**
2   *(KENDRA opens the door. JASON, also mid-twenties and*
3   *wearing a coat, enters and slams the door behind him. He is*
4   *breathing heavily.)*
5 **KENDRA: So, what, did you forget something?**
6 **JASON: No.**
7 **KENDRA: Change your mind?**
8 **JASON: No, and I'm really, really sorry —**
9 **KENDRA: You're shaking.** *(JASON looks at his hand.)*
10 **JASON: Yeah.** *(He holds up his arms, which are shaking.)* **Wow,**
11   **that's pretty bad.** *(KENDRA starts to cry.)* **Look at my arms**
12   **— I can't even stop. My legs, too.**
13 **KENDRA: You can't do this, Jason. You can't just tell me it's over**
14   **without even giving me a reason —**
15 **JASON: I gave you several reasons!**
16 **KENDRA: — without giving me a** *good* **reason, kiss me goodbye**
17   **forever, walk out, and then come running back in!**
18 **JASON: No, that's not it!**
19 **KENDRA: If you're gonna leave me, just** *leave me.*
20 **JASON: But Kay —**
21 **KENDRA: And don't call me that. You can't call me that any**
22   **more.** *(JASON tries to interrupt.)* **And no, you can't spend**
23   **the night.**
24 **JASON: I don't want to spend the night!**
25 **KENDRA: Good!**
26 **JASON: I was shot at.** *(Pause.)*
27 **KENDRA: What?**
28 **JASON: I'm downstairs, and I'm about to leave your building —**
29   **and as soon as I open the door, I hear this sound like an**
30   **explosion, and a** *bullet* **— I mean, it must have been a**
31   **bullet — hit the pavement next to me.**
32 **KENDRA: You were shot at?**
33 **JASON: Yes. You didn't hear the gunshot from in here?**
34 **KENDRA: No. Oh my God, are you serious?**
35 **JASON: Of course I am! Anyway, I don't know what happened,**

1   but I ran back inside. I ran all the way up here. I'm sorry.

2   I know it's awkward timing, but ... I didn't know where

3   else to go. I've never been shot at before.

4   KENDRA: Where did the shot come from?

5   JASON: I don't even know! The street lamp's broken again. God,

6   I hate your neighborhood.

7   KENDRA: Well, you don't have to come here any more. *(Pause.)*

8   Do you want to sit down?

9   JASON: Thanks. *(He sits on the sofa.)* Can I get a glass of water,

10   too? *(KENDRA stares at him from behind, then decides not*

11   *to yell at him.)*

12   KENDRA: Sure. *(She blows her nose and wipes her tears, then*

13   *pours him a glass of water.)*

14   JASON: My heart is like — like I can hear it. And I can feel it in

15   my whole body. It feels like it ought to be moving my shirt.

16   You know what I mean? *(She hands him the glass of water.)*

17   KENDRA: Yes. *(Pause. They stare at each other, holding the glass*

18   *together. Then she lets go. She sits next to him.)*

19   JASON: You really should move. I'm scared to come here at

20   night. I mean, I guess I won't have to, but ... you know, if

21   other people come here at night, they'll be scared, too.

22   *You* should be scared.

23   KENDRA: I like it here. It's nice during the day.

24   JASON: Yeah, but I was shot at.

25   KENDRA: I'm sorry.

26   JASON: I saw an ad yesterday. There are vacancies at the

27   Bridgemont. It's only another hundred a month or so

28   than you're paying now.

29   KENDRA: Why do you care?

30   JASON: Because. I still care about you. Even if we're not

31   together, I don't want anything to happen to you.

32   KENDRA: I can take care of myself. *(JASON takes a long drink of*

33   *water.)*

34   JASON: It's weird, 'cause I thought our conversation was

35   finished, and you probably weren't going to speak to me

1   for awhile. And now ...

2 KENDRA: What.

3 JASON: What?

4 KENDRA: What are you doing?

5 JASON: Nothing. I'm just glad we can still ... talk. You're a great

6   person, Kendra — *(She stands up.)*

7 KENDRA: No. Not again.

8 JASON: I just said you're a great person! *(She gets another*

9   *tissue.)*

10 KENDRA: Don't do this. You already made it clear that we're

11   over. I don't want to start fighting again. *(Pause.)*

12 JASON: Can I take my coat off?

13 KENDRA: How long do you plan on staying?

14 JASON: Kay — Kendra, I almost got killed. Just a few minutes,

15   OK?

16 KENDRA: OK. *(He takes off his coat. Long pause.)*

17 JASON: So. *(Pause. KENDRA looks at JASON, waiting for him to*

18   *continue.)* I'm sorry.

19 KENDRA: You said that already.

20 JASON: It's not you — I just need some time to figure out where

21   I'm going with my life.

22 KENDRA: You said that, too.

23 JASON: I was *shot at*.

24 KENDRA: Were you?

25 JASON: Sorry, it's just ... hard to get over that. I'm still shaking.

26   *(Pause. JASON takes a drink. KENDRA frowns.)*

27 KENDRA: Were you?

28 JASON: Was I what?

29 KENDRA: Shot at.

30 JASON: You think I'm lying? *(KENDRA shrugs.)* I'm not lying.

31   *(Pause.)* Jesus, Kendra, I wouldn't lie about something like

32   that. You're sure you didn't hear the shot? Even with the

33   window open?

34 KENDRA: Positive.

35 JASON: Well, what were you doing when it happened?

1   **KENDRA: Crying.**

2   **JASON: Oh. I'm sor —**

3   **KENDRA: I know.**

4   **JASON: Well, I'm not lying. There was a gunshot, and a bullet**

5   **almost hit me.** *(JASON finishes the water and hands*

6   *KENDRA the glass.)* **Thanks.** *(KENDRA takes the glass to the*

7   *sink.)*

8   **KENDRA: We were good together. I always thought so. I still**

9   **think so.**

10   **JASON: You believe me, right? You know I'm not lying. 'Cause**

11   **the thing is, I really don't feel safe going back out at night**

12   **again. And I don't want you to think I'm pulling**

13   **something — I could sleep on the couch, but —**

14   **KENDRA: You can spend the night if you want.**

15   **JASON: Thank you. I'll leave before you wake up in the**

16   **morning.** *(He exhales.)* **Boy. Wow. My heart is still — I'm**

17   **really shaken. Hey, at least now I can say I've been shot at.**

18   *(Pause.)* **You're really OK with all this? Me spending the**

19   **night?**

20   **KENDRA: I wish you could sleep in the bed.**

21   **JASON: Kay, I can't. It's over. I meant that.**

22   **KENDRA: You could. Just one night. What's the difference?**

23   **JASON: The difference is that ... I mean ...**

24   **KENDRA: Or you don't have to spend the night at all.** *(She*

25   *throws his coat to him.)*

26   **JASON: OK, I'll stay, but really, this was not some plot for me to**

27   **get back into bed with you.** *(KENDRA crosses to him, takes*

28   *the coat back, then stays next to him.)*

29   **KENDRA: I know. Weird how things work out.**

30   **JASON: Yeah. I certainly didn't expect to be sleeping here**

31   **tonight. I thought ... we'd fight, and I'd leave, and that**

32   **would kind of be it.**

33   **KENDRA: Maybe when you set out to hurt someone, but you fail**

34   **... that's love. Think about it.** *(She kisses him. He resists at*

35   *first but then gives in. After a few moments he exits to the*

1   *bedroom and closes the door behind him. As soon as the*
2   *door closes, KENDRA exhales deeply. She crosses to the*
3   *window and closes it. Then she reaches into the potted plant*
4   *and pulls out a revolver. She holds it for a second, then puts*
5   *it into a drawer. She crosses to the bedroom door, opens it,*
6   *and turns out the lights. Blackout.)*

Voices in My Head
by Ry Herman

Pat – Indeterminate age   **Seriocomic**
Sam – Indeterminate age

The following selection can be performed by any gender mix: two women or two men, or a man and a woman in either role. It appears in three sections of this book (scenes for two women, scenes for two men, and scenes for one man and one woman) to fully allow you to read it from all the possible perspectives. Although the scene is quickly read and seems brief, it offers actors plenty of opportunity to play the heartbeats in pauses and silences as Pat suspiciously "considers" the questions that Sam is asking, and Sam gradually discovers the true nature of their relationship. Additionally, the locale is undefined so the actors can explore what kind of environment would best support the action: outdoors on a park bench, in a living room, in an automobile, at the workplace, etc. Like the contentless scenes that are frequently used in acting classes, this scene allows actors to invent and improvise subtext, background and given circumstances, locale, movement, and gesture. The actors should also pay particular attention to the conclusion, deciding whether or not the philosophical impact of the final lines are really a show-stopping conclusion, or if there remains more to be said and done in a subsequent scene between the characters.

1   **PAT:** *(Appearing behind SAM)* **Hi.**

2   **SAM:** *(Startled)* **Pat! Hi.**

3   **PAT: Just came over to see how you were doing.**

4   **SAM: I'm not having a good day, Pat.**

5   **PAT: Sucks to be you.**

6   **SAM: Thanks. Thanks a lot.** *(Pause.)* **Say, Pat?**

7   **PAT: Yeah?**

8   **SAM: You know those voices I keep hearing?**

9   **PAT: Uh-huh?**

1   SAM: They said something totally ludicrous. Want to hear it?

2   PAT: Sure.

3   SAM: They said you were trying to kill me.

4   PAT: Yep. That's pretty ridiculous.

5   SAM: Oh, yeah. I thought so.

6   PAT: I mean, what next?

7   SAM: Exactly. Next they'll be telling me, I don't know …

8   PAT: Your friends are imaginary and the voices are real?

9   SAM: Right, yeah.

10 PAT: You know, this is really a pretty weird conversation.

11 SAM: Ummm. Pat?

12 PAT: Yeah?

13 SAM: How did we meet?

14 PAT: Huh? I don't know. I think we were just hanging around

15   somewhere, or something. Something like that.

16 SAM: Something like that.

17 PAT: Yeah. *(Pause.)* What are you getting at here?

18 SAM: How come I've never seen you enter or leave a room?

19 PAT: What do you mean?

20 SAM: You just appear, or disappear, and I never see you do it.

21 PAT: What?

22 SAM: How about this. Walk through a door.

23 PAT: You're really getting freaky now.

24 SAM: Humor me. Make me feel better. Walk through a door.

25 PAT: I'm not going to encourage this.

26 SAM: Please.

27 PAT: No.

28 SAM: Walk through a door, Pat! *(PAT draws a gun.)* Or not. You

29   don't have to if you really don't want to. That's fine.

30 PAT: I didn't want to have to do this yet.

31 SAM: Pat, come on, put down the gun.

32 PAT: You shouldn't have forced my hand.

33 SAM: Why would you want to kill me? You're my best friend.

34 PAT: Haven't you figured it out yet? I'm not your best friend.

35   I'm not your friend at all.

1   **SAM: Who are you?**
2   **PAT: Oh, come on, think. You know me. You made me.**
3   **SAM: What are you talking about?**
4   **PAT: I'm all in your head. A projection. An alter ego.** *(Pause.*
5   *SAM stares at PAT uncomprehendingly.)* **Multiple personality**
6   **disorder! Man, read a book.**
7   **SAM: So why do you want to kill me?**
8   **PAT: I want your life. You're not using it anyway. So I figure it's**
9   **my turn.**

V-E Day
by Faye Sholiton

Bernie – 22   **Romantic**
Evie – 18

This play is partially set during WWII, when "the greatest generation" pulled together as a nation to fight the Axis powers overseas and on the home front. Evelyn is recalling her youthful days as the editor of a hometown newsletter that she published for the troops, and especially the day when she first met a young student named Bernie who would eventually propose to her. In the original play, this scene is a nostalgic flashback where the older Evelyn regrets her missed opportunities, since at that time in her life she rejected Bernie's proposal. The structure of the scene is very clear, leading step-by-step to the point where the characters kiss. But actors shouldn't overlook the tactful questioning that precedes the climax. The piece also offers opportunities for a certain amount of research into the historical period, especially the way in which women's roles were changing as they took up traditional male occupations on the home front and fully expected men to enlist and do the fighting overseas. Perhaps the most challenging aspect of the scene is the subtext: Bernie is toying with the idea of joining-up instead of going to law school, and Evie is wondering how long this guy is going to be around for the summer.

1   EVIE: Lil tells me you're starting law school.
2   BERNIE: And I walk on water. But enough about me. What
3   about you?
4   EVIE: Just work. Four mornings at a photography studio,
5   downtown. Afternoons and weekends in the x-ray
6   department at Mt. Sinai, for my pop. He's a radiologist.
7   And starting this week, I drive Fridays for the Red Cross.
8   *(Pause.)* But I'm *gonna* be a photojournalist. *(EVIE stops*
9   *stapling.)*
10   BERNIE: What.

1　EVIE: You're not laughing.

2　BERNIE: Did you say something funny? *(Pause.)*

3　EVIE: Here's a good one.

4　BERNIE: *(Reading from newsletter)* "Greetings from Texas,

5　　　where men are men and women are men. So far, I've got a

6　　　desk job and do absolutely nothing. Next week, I'm getting

7　　　an assistant."

8　EVIE: Pretty easy to tell who's still stateside. *(EVIE finds a letter.)*

9　　　This one wants to know to whom he's indebted for his

10　　　subscription.

11　BERNIE: His draft board.

12　EVIE: Mind if I use that?

13　BERNIE: May I? *(BERNIE looks through the mail pile and finds a*

14　　　*letter.)* Jesus. "Air Corps Cadet Albie Lazarus." He was a

15　　　fraternity brother. I didn't know he enlisted ... What?! He's

16　　　gonna be a pilot! Hell, that clown can barely drive a car! I

17　　　once saw him make a U-turn, to the right! ... Huh. Half of

18　　　these have APO addresses already.

19　EVIE: About a third. So how come *you're* not in uniform?

20　BERNIE: What is it with you women and uniforms?

21　EVIE: Why, you 4-F or something?

22　BERNIE: Does this look like a 4-F body?

23　EVIE: You don't need law school, pal. You already answer every

24　　　question with another one.

25　BERNIE: Do I? *(BERNIE resumes his collating task.)*

26　EVIE: So what about this summer? What's doin'?

27　BERNIE: You tell *me*.

28　EVIE: I could use a sports writer. It's lousy wages, but you get all

29　　　the iced tea you can drink.

30　BERNIE: What say we discuss it tonight? Over a burger at

31　　　Mawby's.

32　EVIE: Can't. I'm a hostess at the Stage Door ...

33　BERNIE: Tomorrow, then.

34　EVIE: Pop and I invited a couple of sailors to dinner. You're

35　　　welcome to join us.

1   **BERNIE: What about Thursday?**
2   **EVIE: USO.** *(Pause.)* **Tell you what. Friday. We'll grab some chow**
3   **mein, then do the Statler.** *(EVIE pulls a carnation from the*
4   *vase and makes a boutonniere for BERNIE.)* **Stay right**
5   **there.** *(She puts on music.)* **Gotta see if you can dance.**
6   *(EVIE grabs BERNIE and they dance, in total sync. They dip.)*
7   **Not bad for a 4-F ...**
8   **BERNIE: I'm not a 4-F.**
9   **EVIE: I didn't think you were.** *(They kiss, for several beats. The*
10   *music starts skipping. She breaks away to stop the music.*
11   *She scoops up his glass.)* **Your ice melted.**

Out of Character
by Adam J. Ruben

Man – 20s   Romantic
Woman – 20s

*The following selection is actually a complete ten-minute play, but it
functions equally well as a scene exercise in advanced acting classes
where it can be judiciously cut or used in its entirety. The dialog here
challenges actors to experiment with playing "in" or "out" of their
characters as "Frank" or "Kate," and leads them through a series of
realizations to the biggest one of all — the final moments when they
admit their love to each other. The scene also allows the actors to use
the live audience in a variety of imaginative ways, and can be
effectively staged with no properties or furniture whatsoever.*

1   *(Lights up on a MAN and WOMAN, standing in a bare set.*
2   *The MAN wears a denim jacket, T-shirt, and blue jeans; the*
3   *WOMAN wears what a former era would term a "house*
4   *dress." At the beginning, their speech is deliberately*
5   *melodramatic.)*
6   **MAN: Damn it, Kate! That's it! I'm leaving!** *(The WOMAN grabs*
7   *the MAN's lapels.)*
8   **WOMAN: But Frank! You said you loved me!** *(He shoves her*
9   *aside.)*
10   **MAN: Don't look for me in the garage, baby. I won't be there.**
11   **WOMAN: Frank, no! What about the twins?** *(The MAN grows*
12   *suddenly wistful.)*
13   **MAN: The twins. Growing up without a daddy.** *(Becomes angry*
14   *again.)* **I guess you should have thought about that before**
15   **you** – *(The MAN pauses, entirely floored by an influence*
16   *that is not readily apparent. There is a prolonged silence; it*
17   *is obvious that something has gone wrong.)*

1   **WOMAN:** *(Yelling)* **You're the one** — *(The WOMAN also pauses,*
2   *derailed in the same manner. In silence they both look at*
3   *each other, their faces with normal expressions incongruous*
4   *with the caricatures they had been portraying.)*
5   **MAN:** *(Calmer)* **What's going on?**
6   **WOMAN:** *(Angry)* **Your next line isn't, "What's going on?"** *(She*
7   *gasps.)* **My next line isn't, "Your next line isn't, 'What's**
8   **going on?'"**
9   **MAN: What's going on?**
10 **WOMAN: Stop saying that! That's not in the script!**
11 **MAN: None of this is in the script!**
12 **WOMAN: Shut up! Think of what your next line should have**
13   **been, and say it. Say it now.**
14 **MAN:** *(Pause, a revelation)* **I'm free!**
15 **WOMAN: No, that wasn't it! It was something about the twins.**
16   **Say something about the damn twins!**
17 **MAN:** *(Laughing)* **Twins? You mean the plastic dolls?**
18 **WOMAN:** *(Earnestly trying to resume her character)* **They may be**
19   **plastic, Frank. But they know how to love.**
20 **MAN: That's not a real line either. And it's worse than the lines**
21   **in the play.**
22 **WOMAN: At least I'm trying!**
23 **MAN: Trying to what? I don't get it! One minute we're**
24   **performing a scene** —
25 **WOMAN:** *(Understanding)* **The dialog ran out.** *(She runs to the*
26   *MAN and grabs his shoulders.)*
27 **MAN: What do you mean, "ran out"?**
28 **WOMAN: It ended. It detached. We fell off of it. We lost the**
29   **dialog. Work with me, and maybe we can get back on.**
30 **MAN: I don't want to get back on. It was a stupid play anyway.**
31 **WOMAN: You're being unprofessional. Now start saying lines**
32   **from the play. Maybe no one will notice.**
33 **MAN: Uh-uh. I'm gonna go home now and make myself a**
34   **sandwich. We'll do it right tomorrow.** *(He looks at her*
35   *hands, which grip his shoulders tightly.)* **Ummm ... why are**

1   you grabbing me?

2   WOMAN: I don't want to be grabbing you.

3   MAN: But you are. *(He slaps her, and she turns away.)*

4   WOMAN: You jerk! Why did you slap me?

5   MAN: I didn't!

6   WOMAN: You did! Everyone saw!

7   MAN: I slapped you for the same reason you grabbed me.

8   WOMAN: Why is that?

9   MAN: I have no idea.

10 WOMAN: Oh my God! *(She huddles on the floor as though*

11   *crying.)* I know what happened!

12 MAN: Are you OK?

13 WOMAN: I can't get up.

14 MAN: What's going on?

15 WOMAN: We fell off the dialog ... but not the stage directions.

16 MAN: Stage directions?

17 WOMAN: Don't you remember? This is what Kate does after

18   Frank hits her. She crouches down here and cries.

19 MAN: And what does Frank do?

20 WOMAN: I forget. I never paid attention. *(The MAN walks over*

21   *to the WOMAN; while he's doing so, he looks around*

22   *confusedly — his body has made a decision without*

23   *informing the rest of him.)*

24 MAN: I guess Frank walks over here. *(He puts his hands on his*

25   *hips.)* And then he puts his hands on his hips. *(He notices*

26   *his left hand rising to his forehead and smiles.)* Simon says,

27   put your hand on your forehead. *(His hand stops on his*

28   *forehead; pause. The hand then returns to his hip.)* Simon

29   says, put your hand back on your hip. Now dance around.

30   Very good; Simon didn't say.

31 WOMAN: I can't handle this.

32 MAN: It looks like you have to. *(MAN storms around the stage,*

33   *angrily waving his arms, but talking calmly.)* I think it's

34   kinda fun. I mean, how engaging could the original play

35   have been if we fell out of it?

1   WOMAN: It doesn't matter. I need this play. *(The MAN stops*
2   *storming and puts his hands back on his hips, facing her.)*
3   MAN: For your career?
4   WOMAN: For myself. *(Pause. She rises and points at the MAN.*
5   *She examines the fact that her finger is pointing and tries*
6   *the Kate voice again.)* If you walk out that door, Frank,
7   you're never coming back.
8   MAN: Still me.
9   WOMAN: Damn it!
10 MAN: My costume itches.
11 WOMAN: Well, if Frank doesn't scratch it, you can't scratch it.
12   *(Pause.)* So if Kate was ... what was she ... on the floor, then
13   she points ... what happens next?
14 MAN: Frank apologizes to the audience and waits out the rest
15   of the play. *(To audience)* Sorry, folks. We appear to be
16   having technical difficulties. I don't know what the deal is
17   with refunds –
18 WOMAN: No! You always do this! You play around, you don't
19   care about the show, or any of the cast –
20 MAN: The cast is just you! *(The WOMAN grabs her own breasts.)*
21 WOMAN: Can't you take this seriously for just one line?
22 MAN: Why are you grabbing your breasts?
23 WOMAN: I wish I knew. Look, just say one line of the play. One.
24   I'll say a line, then you say a line. *(The WOMAN lets go of*
25   *her breasts and crosses to the MAN. He retreats somewhat.)*
26 MAN: But we don't have the lines.
27 WOMAN: Try!
28 MAN: *(As Frank)* Ummm ... Kate, I'm sorry things didn't work
29   out.
30 WOMAN: *(As Kate)* Oh, Frank! Hold me! *(Pause.)*
31 MAN: *(Himself)* Yet I'm still over here.
32 WOMAN: *(As Kate)* Frank? Please, hold me? *(The MAN starts*
33   *taking off his jacket.)*
34 MAN: Frank's taking off his jacket now. Frank doesn't know
35   why.

1   WOMAN: *(Herself)* **You stopped trying.**

2   MAN: **Give it up. We lost the dialog. We're stuck. We're stuck**

3   **until the play ends.** *(The MAN turns his back on the*

4   *WOMAN and paces back and forth, looking at his legs*

5   *periodically, which seem to be moving of their own accord.*

6   *The WOMAN throws herself to the floor, also against her*

7   *will.)*

8   WOMAN: *(Calling from the floor)* **That's what I need, though. I**

9   **need that ending. The end of the play.**

10 MAN: *(From over his shoulder)* **Why?**

11 WOMAN: **I don't remember.** *(She begins writhing on the floor,*

12   *moving her arms as if during impassioned speech.)*

13 MAN: **Well, whatever it is, we'll be doing it.**

14 WOMAN: **We'll be doing it. Not Kate and Frank.**

15 MAN: **Does that scare you?**

16 WOMAN: **Yes! I don't know what's going to happen!**

17 MAN: **Come on. Smile. We'll finish this thing together. It'll**

18   **make a funny story tonight at the diner.** *(The MAN throws*

19   *his jacket to the ground. The WOMAN picks it up.)*

20 WOMAN: **You still want to go to the diner after the show?**

21 MAN: **Why not?**

22 WOMAN: **Because we might run into someone from the**

23   **audience.** *(She tries to give him back his jacket.)*

24 MAN: **So what?**

25 WOMAN: **So what? They can see me! Me, me!**

26 MAN: **Me too. And I don't mind.** *(He throws the jacket back on the*

27   *floor and stomps on it during the following. To the*

28   *audience)* **Hi. I'm thirty-five years old. I still play carnival**

29   **games, even if I'm not trying to win the stuffed animal for**

30   **someone else. I cried during *The Land Before Time*, and if**

31   **I could have dinner with anyone tonight, it would be my**

32   **mother.**

33 WOMAN: **Good for you. You're endearing.**

34 MAN: **My point is that I'm pathetic.** *(The WOMAN picks up his*

35   *jacket and caresses it.)*

1   **WOMAN: You're endearing. I'm pathetic.** *(Pause.)* **This jacket is**
2   **filthy.**
3   **MAN: You know what? I think you enjoy being Kate.**
4   **WOMAN: Of course I do; I'm an actress.** *(The MAN snatches his*
5   *jacket from the WOMAN and throws it Off-stage.)*
6   **MAN: No, I mean I think you like being downtrodden. Having**
7   **an excuse to be so neurotic. All your own fears get smaller**
8   **when you're constantly worried about Frank and the**
9   **twins.**
10 **WOMAN: The twins are plastic.**
11 **MAN: I know.** *(Pause. The MAN takes a step closer to the*
12   *WOMAN.)* **You want this ending for Kate.**
13 **WOMAN: I want to see that everything works out for her.** *(The*
14   *WOMAN takes a step towards the MAN. During the next few*
15   *lines, they move closer to each other.)*
16 **MAN: But she's not real.**
17 **WOMAN: She's a symbol.**
18 **MAN: You're real. Take the ending for yourself.**
19 **WOMAN: No one wants to see me do this. They want to see Kate.**
20   **Kate is a deep character with dimensions and feelings.**
21   *(The MAN embraces the WOMAN from behind, with his*
22   *arms around her waist. He notices what he's doing with*
23   *astonishment but uses the action to propel his next line.)*
24 **MAN: I just want to see you do this. You're a million times as**
25   **deep as Kate because ... you're real. Just keep being**
26   **yourself until the end.**
27 **WOMAN:** *(Straining to look back at him)* **It's not like I have a**
28   **choice, is it?** *(She smiles.)* **You are endearing.**
29 **MAN:** *(Also smiling)* **You are pathetic.** *(Pause. Suddenly the MAN*
30   *is struck by the same expression as in the beginning of the*
31   *play.)*
32 **WOMAN: What's wrong?**
33 **MAN:** *(As Frank)* **You may be pathetic, Kate, but you know I**
34   **would never leave you.**
35 **WOMAN:** *(Herself)* **I'm not Kate.**

1 **MAN:** *(Still Frank)* **And I would never leave the twins.**

2 **WOMAN: I'm not Kate.**

3 **MAN:** *(Himself, whispering)* **You can step back in if you want. I**

4   **think I've found the dialog.**

5 **WOMAN: That's OK.**

6 **MAN: You don't want to be Kate?** *(The WOMAN faces the MAN*

7   *and throws her arms around his neck. She notices this*

8   *before speaking but speaks as though glad of her actions.)*

9 **WOMAN: And I don't want you to be Frank.** *(They kiss.*

10   *Blackout.)*

None of the Above
by Jenny Lyn Bader

Jamie – 17   **Romantic Comedy**
Clark – 23

This charming extract from a much longer scene is built upon sharp character contrasts that the actors need to achieve: Jamie, an over-privileged, under-supervised teenager; and Clark, the tutor her father has hired. This first encounter between them soon erupts into fireworks, but develops by the end into a greater mutual understanding — perhaps even the basis for love. The actors should therefore be attentive here to discoveries, conclusions, and decisions their characters make during the scene. The actors should also be sure to play a strong subtext to the scene: Clark may be just as fascinated by Jamie's lifestyle as he is by her academic indifference; and Jamie might be just as preoccupied with Clark's motives for staying as she is with avoiding his tutorial instructions. While the actors must sustain the comedy here that bubbles moment-by-moment, they must also be sure that they end up with a different outlook at the end of the scene than the way they began. And that their relationship expresses real chemistry.

1   (*JAMIE is alone in her lavish bedroom, smoking and doing*
2   *her nails simultaneously, while dancing to electrifying pop*
3   *music. She blows cigarette smoke on her nails to dry them,*
4   *then dances around the room. A completed game of solitaire*
5   *looms on her computer screen. There is a knocking on the*
6   *door that gets louder and more insistent until she realizes*
7   *someone is at the door. She puts out the cigarette, lowers the*
8   *music, grabs her purse, and opens the door.*)
9   **JAMIE: You're late!**
10 **CLARK: What?** (*JAMIE turns the music off.*)
11 **JAMIE: You're late.**

1   CLARK: Actually, I'm five minutes early. Hi, I'm Clark.

2   JAMIE: Your *name* is Clark?

3   CLARK: Is that a problem?

4   JAMIE: You're not early, you're late. I believe you were
5   supposed to be here at five thirty, and it's five fifty-five.
6   But let's not argue over details. Have you got everything?

7   CLARK: I'm supposed to be here at six, and I don't know what
8   you mean by "everything." I've got the books.

9   JAMIE: Books?

10   CLARK: Let's start again. You're Jamie. I'm Clark, your SAT
11   tutor.

12   JAMIE: Oh, shit! I totally forgot.

13   CLARK: You mean you *utterly* forgot.

14   JAMIE: I thought you were someone else. Utterly. You want a
15   beer?

16   CLARK: No, thanks. I usually don't *imbibe* on the job.

17   JAMIE: Right. Wouldn't want to get – er – inebriated?

18   CLARK: Very good! *(JAMIE rolls her eyes.)* Did you know, too
19   much beer can be *dehydrating*? *(She takes out a bottle of*
20   *Evian.)*

21   JAMIE: Well, I always have water around.

22   CLARK: *(Surprised)* You know *dehydrating*?

23   JAMIE: It's a rather common word.

24   CLARK: You got it wrong on your PSAT.

25   JAMIE: Did I? Funny. *(Pause.)* Wait. How the hell do you know
26   that?

27   CLARK: Well, for an appointed sum of money, you can request
28   the exact answers and questions of a given student and ...

29   JAMIE: And my father bought it.

30   CLARK: Yes, he did.

31   JAMIE: How much is he paying you?

32   CLARK: I'm not at liberty to say. So – you know the word
33   *dehydrating*, yet you got it wrong on the test. Explain why
34   in fifty words or less.

35   JAMIE: *(Smiles.)* I was wasted out of my mind during the test.

1   My friend, Justine, she was mad about there being a test?
2   So she like rented out the Twenty-one Club the night
3   before ... I think that was less than fifty words.
4   CLARK: It was thirty-three words. Very nice.
5   JAMIE: You just made that up. You could *not* have counted.
6   CLARK: *(Rapidly)* "I was wasted out of my mind during the
7   test." Ten words. "My friend Justine she was mad about
8   there being a test." Eleven words. "So she like rented out
9   the Twenty-one Club the night before." Twelve words,
10   including "like" used incorrectly but we'll throw it in. Ten
11   plus eleven plus twelve last I checked is thirty-three. So
12   no, I didn't make it up.
13   JAMIE: Where did you learn to do that?
14   CLARK: Unfortunately, I always knew. So — *(Still grappling with*
15   *this)* — your friend Justine rented a *room* at the Twenty-
16   one Club?
17   JAMIE: No. The whole restaurant. After hours. Private party.
18   So, yeah, we stayed out late that night.
19   CLARK: Wow. And you were hung over during the test?
20   JAMIE: Not sure. No, I think I never went to bed. I think I was
21   still drunk.
22   CLARK: That's great!
23   JAMIE: It is?
24   CLARK: You could raise your score immediately, just by taking
25   the SAT sober.
26   JAMIE: Maybe.
27   CLARK: Maybe? Jamie, you didn't know this was one-third! *(He*
28   *shows her a pie chart. She laughs.)*
29   JAMIE: I hate those pie things.
30   CLARK: They're called pie charts. And they're just circles.
31   Perfect circles, divided into precise, vivid morsels. Each
32   one unique. What is there to hate about them?
33   JAMIE: *(Mystified)* How can you care so much about circles?
34   CLARK: How can you not?
35   JAMIE: Have you considered getting help for that? What might

1   it mean that you're so into circles?

2   CLARK: It might mean I like abstract renderings of fractions.

3   JAMIE: Look, it's nice that you appreciate the pie things.

4   Charts. Whatever. But studying is not a good context for

5   me to meet people in. Studying is just not *me*. So why

6   don't you leave?

7   CLARK: What?

8   JAMIE: I'll tell them you came and tutored me. And you can just

9   take the money and run.

10 CLARK. I can't leave. I have a job to do.

11 JAMIE: Consider it done.

12 CLARK: But I want to do it. I care about doing it.

13 JAMIE: Right. You're here because you care deeply about me.

14 CLARK: I care *profoundly* about your test score. I hope that we

15   can *augment* it in our sessions together.

16 JAMIE: "Augment it"? Do you always talk like this?

17 CLARK: I talk like this with my students.

18 JAMIE: You know what I think? I think you always talk like this

19   — with your students ... with your friends, if you have any.

20   I think you couldn't stop if you wanted to. And I think you

21   always count words, too. No matter who you're talking to.

22   You can't help it. *(Pause.)* How many was that?

23 CLARK: Forty-nine.

24 JAMIE: See what I mean?

25 CLARK: While you, on the other hand, don't even bother

26   counting when you're supposed to. Your Math PSAT —

27   four-eighty. I know you were drunk at the time, but it's

28   still not encouraging.

29 JAMIE: Math isn't my favorite subject.

30 CLARK: What do you mean by that?

31 JAMIE: Is that a trick question? It's boring.

32 CLARK: Take this problem. Greg and Hilda are grading papers.

33   There are forty students in their class. Eighty-five percent

34   of the students do not receive A's. How many receive an A?

35 *(She pauses, as if about to answer.)*

1   JAMIE: The question is ridiculous. It's not like it's a situation
2   you're going to run into very often. Who are Greg and
3   Hilda? Especially Hilda. No one today is named Hilda. No
4   one would dare name their child Hilda. And why do two
5   people have to grade papers for only forty students?
6   Schools are understaffed enough as it is. One teacher
7   should be able to handle forty papers. And eighty-five
8   percent of the kids not getting an A? That means like,
9   what, fifteen percent A's? That's unusual. It's not a lot.
10   Why are they giving so few A's? They don't seem like very
11   nice people.
12   CLARK: Why don't you just tell me the answer.
13   JAMIE: Twelve.
14   CLARK: That's not the answer.
15   JAMIE: It isn't?
16   CLARK: *(Interested)* Why do you say twelve?
17   JAMIE: Because the answer tends to be twelve. Believe me. If
18   you answer twelve often enough you do pretty well.
19   CLARK: Do you know how to calculate fifteen percent?
20   JAMIE: I don't think you appreciate how right I am about the
21   nature of twelve. My friend Bill and I figured it out in the
22   sixth grade, and it has helped us through many a trying
23   time.
24   CLARK: Well, I'm in linguistics graduate school, and I can
25   promise you the answer is never twelve.
26   JAMIE: That's your fault for studying linguistics. *(The phone*
27   *rings.)* Excuse me. Hello? Hi! Yeah, Friday. The Clash Club.
28   Only rule is you have to wear something that clashes. Well,
29   of course, it can be designed by Jane's mom, just don't tell
30   her. *(To CLARK)* The children of all New York City fashion
31   designers attend Billington. It's very stressful. *(Back to*
32   *SHEILA)* No one. Family friend. So what I want to know is
33   did you actually get academic credit for baking those
34   cookies? What did you tell Madame Vernelle? French
35   cookies? Omigod, from Proust? Too much. Mmmmm-

1   hmmmm. All my love. Later. *(She hangs up.)* That was
2   Sheila Martin. A horrible, vindictive, superficial girl, with
3   no spiritual values or social graces, and the biggest moron
4   ever to roam the earth. Sorry. You were saying? *(CLARK
5   stares at JAMIE's bracelet. He gestures towards it.)*
6   CLARK: What kind of triangle is that? *(JAMIE glances at it.)*
7   JAMIE: What kind of triangle? It's a bracelet.
8   CLARK: Yes, and ...
9   JAMIE: And ... it's a silver triangle.
10 CLARK: Is it — equilateral? Scalene?
11 JAMIE: Looks like sterling silver.
12 CLARK: It's an isosceles triangle. Do you know why?
13 JAMIE: Because of its shape.
14 CLARK: Right! Can you explain that?
15 JAMIE: I don't need to explain it. I just need to fill the circle,
16   right? They don't want explanations.
17 CLARK: I want explanations.
18 JAMIE: Ummm ... two sides are the same, the third side
19   different.
20 CLARK: Good!
21 JAMIE: *(Changing the subject)* I have triangle earrings, too, with
22   all the sides different.
23 CLARK: *(Returning to the subject)* And your earrings are —
24 JAMIE: They're copper with a cubic zirconium stone?
25 CLARK: But are they — isoceles?
26 JAMIE: *(Exhausted)* No.
27 CLARK: They are ...
28 JAMIE: Clip-ons.
29 CLARK: They're scalene. If you see triangles that look like your
30   copper clip-on earrings on the test ...
31 JAMIE: I fill in the circle that says "scalene."
32 CLARK: Does any of this seem at all familiar to you?
33 JAMIE: Sure, I just don't know why anyone would care. *(A knock
34   on the door.)* Excuse me. *(Opening the door and addressing
35   someone Off-stage)* You're late. You sure it's good? Cool.

1   **Right. Later.** *(Returning with a wad of bills and a paper bag.)*
2   **Sorry.**
3 CLARK: Great. So you're on drugs, too.
4 JAMIE: Are you kidding? I've totally quit. I don't even smoke
5   any more. Besides cigarettes.
6 CLARK: So what was that?
7 JAMIE: I deal a little. I need the money.
8 CLARK: *(Looking around the room)* You? Need the money?
9 JAMIE: My parents won't give me money any more? Not since
10   this party I gave where I ... broke this Ming vase thing and
11   they said it would come out of my allowance and I
12   wouldn't see my trust fund 'til I'm thirty. So I looked at my
13   savings and thought, hey, in not many communities
14   would a few hundred dollars be serious cash flow, but in
15   high school? I could be the connection girl. I can advance
16   it, then take a little cut.
17 CLARK: What's a little cut?
18 JAMIE: Fifteen percent.
19 CLARK: We just had a problem with fifteen percent!
20 JAMIE: Did we?
21 CLARK: OK. Solve this. Guy sells you some weed. He charges
22   you forty dollars. You sell it to the next guy and take your
23   usual cut. How much do you earn?
24 JAMIE: Six bucks.
25 CLARK: Yes! And it's not twelve bucks, is it! It's six bucks.
26 JAMIE: Why would it be twelve?
27 CLARK: You said it's the answer to everything.
28 JAMIE: On *tests*. Not in business. When you talk about Greg and
29   Hilda, I start to zone out. It's not the same as doing a deal.
30 CLARK: You'd prefer if the questions on the SAT involved
31   illegal transactions?
32 JAMIE: Oh, come on. You know drugs should be legalized.
33   You're a graduate student.
34 CLARK: Actually, I don't think drugs should be legalized. You
35   should be more careful.

1 JAMIE: What do you mean? Like safe sex?
2 CLARK: I mean scheduling your deal during your tutoring
3   session. It's desperate behavior. It's as if you want to be
4   caught.
5 JAMIE: No, wanting to be caught is for hardened criminals.
6   This was more a case of being double-booked.
7 CLARK: Double-booked.
8 JAMIE: Don't you ever schedule two activities at once? The
9   school play, the weekend class trip to France?
10 CLARK: You had a "weekend class trip" to France?
11 JAMIE: I've been plagued by double-booking from the age of
12   eleven. Please don't mention this to my parents. I really
13   thought you would be cool about it. Just from your general
14   ... coolness?
15 CLARK: You know I have no general coolness.
16 JAMIE: Sure you do. Well ... you have glimpses. Of coolness.
17   *(CLARK takes out a copy of* The New York Times.*)* **What are**
18   **you doing?** *The New York Times* **is a conspiracy. I never**
19   **read it.**
20 CLARK: Do you see any words on page one that you don't know?
21 JAMIE: I see words everywhere I don't know. That's not why I
22   don't read it. It's dirty, it comes off on your hands. *(She*
23   *watches, fascinated, as he spreads the newspaper out in*
24   *front of her.)* **You really do care about my score, don't you?**
25 CLARK: Yeah.
26 JAMIE: Wait! My father's paying you on a sliding scale, isn't he?
27   Depending on how well I do. He's paying you more the
28   higher I score, isn't he? Just tell me that.
29 CLARK: Jamie, I need to warn you about fixating on the dollar
30   as your only way of interpreting situations and making
31   decisions. It's a mistake I've made, and it ends badly.
32 JAMIE: So he *is*! He *is* paying you on a sliding scale! And that's
33   why you're doing it. It's OK. I'm just trying to understand.
34 CLARK: Has it occurred to you I might enjoy tutoring you? Or
35   you might enjoy taking the test? Derive pleasure from it?

1 JAMIE: No. The test means doing something you hate in order
2   to do something you love.
3 CLARK: What do you love?
4 JAMIE: *That* is none of your business.
5 CLARK: But you love something?
6 JAMIE: Doing something you hate in order to do something you
7   love goes against my loving nature. And I am very loving.
8   Usually. But with stuff I hate, frankly, I'm very hating.
9   Even more hating than loving. I warn you.
10 CLARK: You're warning me.
11 JAMIE: I admit I'm in no position to warn you, because now
12   that you know I deal drugs, you could blackmail me, you
13   could destroy me.
14 CLARK: Do you often give people the tools to destroy you?
15 JAMIE: You must know my ex-boyfriend. Have you ever tutored
16   anyone at Billington before?
17 CLARK: No. I've never had a private student.
18 JAMIE: Omigod! You're not even qualified to teach me!

The Story of the Panda Bears Told by a Saxophonist Who Has a Girlfriend in Frankfurt
by Matéi Visniec

Him — 20s   **Romantic Comedy**
Her — 20s

This challenging selection requires strong nonverbal communication skills, particularly from the male actor who has only one word to speak: "Ah." Because of this, it's an excellent scene to use for exploring relationships and scene structure. It also leaves a great deal to the actors' imaginations because the locale, the ages of the characters, the costumes, and the characters' backgrounds are non-specific. In fact, even the gender of the two characters can be fluid. Almost like a "contentless scene," the piece allows the actors to shape the encounter in different ways: as a love relationship, a simple friendship, a therapy session, or in other terms. Perhaps its most challenging feature is the way that it develops elliptically toward a very clear ending to the relationship from the way it began: soundless communication or ESP between the characters. Thus the actors need to work together imaginatively in order to structure the way in which the dialog develops, or the scene will seem to wander and lose focus as the dialog proceeds.

1   **HER: Say "ah."**
2   **HIM: Ah.**
3   **HER: More tenderly: "ah."**
4   **HIM: Ah.**
5   **HER: Whisper: "ah."**
6   **HIM: Ah.**
7   **HER: I want a soft "ah."**
8   **HIM: Ah.**
9   **HER: Loud but soft: "ah."**

1   HIM: Ah.

2   HER: Say "ah" as if to say you love me.

3   HIM: Ah.

4   HER: Say "ah" as if to say you will never forget me.

5   HIM: Ah.

6   HER: Say "ah" as if to say you think I'm beautiful.

7   HIM: Ah.

8   HER: Say "ah" as if to say you are bloody stupid!

9   HIM: Ah.

10 HER: Say "ah" as if to say you want me.

11 HIM: Ah.

12 HER: Say "ah" as if to say: "Stay!"

13 HIM: Ah.

14 HER: Say "ah" as if to say: "Get undressed!"

15 HIM: Ah.

16 HER: Say "ah" as if you were asking me why I am late.

17 HIM: Ah.

18 HER: Say "ah" to say hello to me.

19 HIM: Ah.

20 HER: Say "ah" to say goodbye to me.

21 HIM: Ah.

22 HER: Say "ah" to ask me if I have brought you something.

23 HIM: Ah.

24 HER: Say "ah" to tell me that you're happy.

25 HIM: Ah.

26 HER: Say "ah" to tell me that you never want to see me again.

27 HIM: Ah.

28 HER: No, that's not right ...

29 HIM: Ah!

30 HER: Look, if you don't do exactly as I say, I'll stop the game ...

31 HIM: Ah.

32 HER: Good. Say "ah" as if you were saying that you never

33   wanted to see me again.

34 HIM: Ah.

35 HER: Very good. Now, say "ah" as if you were telling me that

1   **you slept very badly without me, that you dreamt only of**
2   **me, and that you woke up exhausted with no desire to**
3   **carry on living.**
4 **HIM: Ah.**
5 **HER: Hmmmm. Say "ah" to tell me that you have something**
6   **really important to tell me.**
7 **HIM: Ah.**
8 **HER: Say "ah" to tell me to stop asking you to say "ah."**
9 **HIM: Ah.**
10 **HER: Say "ah" to say how wonderful it is to talk only in "ah."**
11 **HIM: Ah.**
12 **HER: Ask me to say "ah."**
13 **HIM: Ah.**
14 **HER: Ask me to say a soft "ah."**
15 **HIM: Ah.**
16 **HER: Ask me to say a soft whispering "ah."**
17 **HIM: Ah.**
18 **HER: Ask me if I love you as much as you love me.**
19 **HIM: Ah ... ?**
20 **HER: Tell me that I'm driving you crazy.**
21 **HIM: Ah!**
22 **HER: And that you've had enough!**
23 **HIM: Ah!**
24 **HER: OK ... Do I want a coffee?**
25 **HIM: Ah?**
26 **HER: Yes, I'd love one.** *(He gets up and pours her a cup of coffee.)*
27 **HIM: Ah?**
28 **HER: Just a small piece, thank you.** *(He hands her his cigarette*
29   *packet.)*
30 **HIM: Ah?**
31 **HER: No, thank you, I have my own.** *(She takes out a packet of*
32   *cigarettes and takes one.)*
33 **HIM:** *(Offering her a light)* **Ah?**
34 **HER: No, not just yet.**
35 **HIM: Ah?**

1   HER: I don't know ... Though I think I prefer to eat at home.
2   HIM: Ah.
3   HER: All right. But do we have any sauce?
4   HIM: Ah.
5   HER: We'll go out then.
6   HIM: Ah!
7   HER: We'll stay in then.
8   HIM: Ah ...
9   HER: Come here.
10 HIM: Ah ...
11 HER: Look me straight in the eyes.
12 HIM: Ah.
13 HER: Say "ah" in your mind.
14 HIM: ...
15 HER: Softer.
16 HIM: ...
17 HER: Louder. And clearer so I can catch it.
18 HIM: ...
19 HER: Now, say "ah" in your mind as if to say you love me ...
20 HIM: ...
21 HER: Once again.
22 HIM: ...
23 HER: Say "ah" in your mind as if to say you'll never forget me.
24 HIM: ...
25 HER: Say "ah" in your mind as if to say you think I'm beautiful.
26 HIM: ...
27 HER: And now I'm going to ask you something ... Something
28   very important ... And you're going to answer in your
29   mind. Are you ready?
30 HIM: ...
31 HER: Ah?
32 HIM: ...
33 HER: ...
34 HIM: ...
35 HER: ...

Monologs
for Women

Missing Dan Nolan
by Mark Wheeller

Sarah – Teens   **Serious**

Although this monolog seems to dwell on the past as a quiet narration, its real strength lies in Sarah's present struggle to grapple with the uncertainty, the tragedy, and the unsettling feelings that continue to torment her. It offers the actress several key choices to make in order to present the piece effectively: the identity of Sarah's vis-à-vis, the deeper relationship between Sarah and Dan that lies unexpressed beneath the lines, or the nature of Sarah's vague fear and dread that something of the sort might happen to her or to others. There is also a range of emotion possible to express here: Sarah's impatience with her classmates' reactions to Dan's disappearance, her struggle to put her own tangled feelings into words (note the fragmented speech pattern in several key locations), the half-hearted attempt to put some closure on the experience at the very end, and of course, her sadness and puzzlement over what really happened to Dan Nolan.

1 SARAH: I knew nothing about Dan's disappearance until the
2   afternoon of January the second. Mum was driving me
3   home from dancing. The news came on ... it was a lady ...
4   she said something like ... a Hampshire boy has gone
5   missing. Then ... "Daniel Nolan." I felt like everything in
6   my body had gone completely dead. Back at school
7   everyone tried hard to act normal ... but it was ... you didn't
8   know what to ... you didn't ... know what to say ... like, do
9   you talk about him in the past or in the present? Some
10   people were saying he'd been drinking ... no one had that
11   image of Dan ... I was really surprised. I've never heard the
12   Crush Hall be so quiet for an assembly ... ever. Our priest
13   said we must pray for his family. It was the longest prayer

1   we've ever had ... there were a couple of sniffles in the
2   audience ... I was crying ... I'll admit that ... a couple of
3   people had to walk out. The whole place was so somber.
4   That math book of Dan's that I borrowed ... I've still got it
5   ... so it stays in my locker now ... it's just a little memory of
6   him, I wouldn't want to lose that. People didn't like
7   talking about Dan while he was missing ... they said it
8   upset them. I found that really depressing ... it made me
9   think that they were kind of forgetting him. I'll remember
10   the little things ... like him swinging on his chair or doing
11   homework in the group bases ... which is forbidden ...
12   because homework, as the teachers say, is for home. I'll
13   remember his sense of humour and his smile ... I'll
14   remember him making me laugh. I won't ever forget Dan
15   Nolan.

The Doe
by Elise Geither

Tomlyn — 20s   Serious

This monolog permits the actress to explore mystery and secret, creating a strong mood of suspense and dread as Tomlyn recounts her encounter with the ghost. It also allows the actress to invent a range of possibilities for playing the scene: the identity of the dead woman, the speaker's relationship with the ghost, the unspoken words that Tomlyn confesses she should have shared with the ghost when she was once alive, and the identity of Tomlyn's vis-à-vis. Finally, the actress should be sensitive to the range of emotions that Tomlyn expresses here because her words are not simply filled with awe, fear, and menace. Tomlyn also beats herself up for her failure to speak openly with the dead spirit when she was alive, mentions her weariness in having to deal with this nightmare again and again, expresses her frustration at her inability to communicate with the ghost, and struggles to resolve the problem with the help of her vis-à-vis. In its overall structure, the monolog begs for some resolution, some decision or insight at the conclusion, leaving the actress several rich possibilities for ending the piece effectively.

1   TOMLYN: It's happened twice. People don't just leave. Two
2   people don't just leave. That night, I dreamt about her
3   again. I think I'm awake and I'm walking down the hall to
4   the bathroom. And the lights go on. Everywhere. I'm
5   frozen for a second, then sneak to the doorway. My hair
6   hangs behind me like a sheet, a waterfall. I see her. She's
7   moving, slow motion, through water, down the hall. She is
8   ghostly, and I feel my skin prickle. She's moving down the
9   hall and lightly touching each door and they spring open
10 at her touch. She looks into each room and she is
11 confused. She is looking for something or someone. I'm
12 still frozen but know I should talk to her. But what else

1   can I say? I've daydreamed this a hundred times, seeing
2   her, talking. Telling her all my secrets, everything I should
3   have told her over the years. Or just touching her, making
4   sure she is real. I notice something moving at her feet, a
5   dark wave. I look closer and see it's my hair, my waterfall
6   of hair has hit the floor and is flowing to her like dark
7   cream. She looks down, but it's too late and my hair has
8   touched her, tentatively at first, like a cat. Then,
9   recognizing her, it coils once, twice, again and again
10   around her legs. She gives a slight smile, but the hair must
11   have tightened because the smile fails and she looks
12   panicked. The hair keeps flowing and it's all around her.
13   Like a cocoon.

120 Lives a Minute
by Gustavo Ott, translated by Heather L. McKay

Emily – Indeterminate age   **Seriocomic**

*This extended monolog presents several creative challenges to the
actress who must track the stream of Emily's thoughts as she
contemplates her career as a stewardess on one of her routine flights.
For example, there are numerous points in the text where the actress
can decide upon what major beats to play in the monolog; what
emotional emphases she wishes to make, and what pace would be
appropriate in the different sections. Additionally, there are no stage
directions to limit the actress's choice of physical actions: is she
standing throughout while preparing a beverage tray? Or is she
sitting and moving around at any point — perhaps even moving up
and down the aisle while speaking? Most importantly, the actress
must avoid presenting the monolog as simply an idle stream of
consciousness that passes the time; instead she must find strong
reasons why Emily feels that she absolutely must share her thoughts
with the audience here and now.*

1   EMILY: My feet hurt because they make us wear heels, or else
2   they screw you. The granite tray was heavy, the passenger
3   in Three-F in first class just asked for another whiskey and
4   I'm already sleepwalking tired, I'm ready to throw myself
5   from thirty-thousand feet up in the air or to fall asleep
6   stock-still without moving, right here, because this tray's
7   sharp and heavy, my feet hurt and mistakes aren't long,
8   not in coming at this point, but in serving as my only
9   excuse to rest, by shutting myself in the bathroom, the
10   cockpit, cut to bits by the stainless steel boxes on the food
11   cart. If there was someone to feel sorry for me, someone to
12   want to stop looking at me, someone to not call me,
13   someone to fall asleep, someone to look out the window

1	and his soul lights up, that's right, his soul, any soul,
2	whatever soul, *the neophyte, blind, ignorant soul*, or
3	whatever kind of soul, for him to be moved to it or invent
4	it while looking out at the clouds, it's night, but the clouds
5	are still there, for someone to see the invisible clouds,
6	invisible friends, and the night lights up for that
7	passenger and then, from the wonder of seeing what can't
8	be seen through the half-open window, from seeing the
9	stars so close and definitively just as far, waiting for the
10	sun to swell or blossom, and at this height the sun always
11	seems tired, on the same side, and suddenly, as if the sun
12	had a memory and knew it all or instead it's an amnesiac
13	sun that only repeats itself because it doesn't remember if
14	it had one life or many, it didn't have one, it didn't have
15	any, not even this one, like the guy whose leg was
16	amputated and he thinks he felt it but he doesn't feel it
17	anymore. That passenger sees me seeing him and looks at
18	my legs ... *(She laughs)* ... my legs, and he thinks they're
19	paltry, these two stainless steel posts broken by more than
20	one hundred twenty collisions and flight hours, and he
21	sees my legs riddled with bullet holes in the miserable
22	fantasy of a passenger who no longer looks out the
23	window at the clouds, the night, and the stars, but also
24	comes and looks at my shapeless legs, these
25	parallelepiped legs, if he knew how they hurt, if he knew
26	the colors they spill, the lines intersecting them, and he
27	looks at these legs that no one has looked at in two
28	hundred years and that don't work besides and that fall
29	asleep walking and where I've thought not even blood
30	flows, instead, in my acrophobic legs, battery water
31	circulates, or oil for the hinges on the gate holding back
32	the refuse, filthy gate and filthy liquid to keep these
33	invalid legs from squeaking, with their invalid
34	personality, because, with everything, really, they squeal,
35	they squeal like an oil drill and that prepackaged

1   passenger, so ready and served, who never stops thinking
2   that I'm here on the wall, stamped on the flight valet, that
3   I'm put here, hung, like a sample, inflatable, electronic,
4   penetrable, at his service, pushed, a stop light, screwed in,
5   welded to the emergency door, because that's what I am,
6   the emergency door, I am the emergency, the emergency
7   opens the door and colors his world, reads magazines and
8   serves him dinner, his breakfast, his whiskey, his life
9   jacket, his emergency door with a wide buckle, XXL, or
10 narrower, if you please, as you wish, an emergency
11 stewardess who decorates his visa, his boarding pass, his
12 handicapped headphones, me, the same Cheez-filled me,
13 the one who slips away in people's pockets. Me, the one
14 who hangs from the pleated skirt, the one who is always
15 checked and re-checked with her turbo heavy tray and her
16 one without the other feet, with her feet on the tray or
17 sometimes the tray at her feet, because they make us wear
18 heels, or else they screw you. He looks at my legs, calls me
19 over, asks for his whiskey, calls me honey and he doesn't
20 even know who I am. He doesn't know who I am, and he
21 doesn't know that this is my last flight either. This is my
22 last flight because I am what I am. I could have been a
23 florist or a receptionist, a secretary, a salesgirl in a
24 bookstore or a warehouse, or anywhere. I thought about it
25 on the weekends and even on Thursdays, at the beach,
26 with the windsurfing, kite surfing, mountain climbing,
27 parasailing, bungee jumping, in the discos, with the boys
28 and their broken glass smiles. Then I started to have
29 rapid-fire fainting fits, I'd faint full of holes at three in the
30 morning, revive and then faint off again at three-thirty,
31 more or less every day, after my thirteenth beer and
32 fourth snort of whatever. Then, I'd fall flat out, just as long
33 and lean, wherever the attack would hit me and there was
34 always some feral friend willing to take me to his house, to
35 strip me so I wouldn't sleep in my clothes, to sleep with

1   me so I'd feel warm, passed from man to man, maybe not
2   even that, because all it took was for someone to slide up
3   to me between the lights and the canned music and then
4   pick me up off the floor and take me, without much
5   pretense, or even hiding it, like someone picking up
6   change, because they understood, I don't know how or in
7   what language, that a woman's groan for help or a twenty-
8   year-old gagging is, of course, an invitation for sex. It
9   couldn't be disgust. Or contempt. I stopped going out with
10   my panther friends and they forgot about me the next day.
11   And I thought: "No one knows me, no one cares about me.
12   I could go ahead and kill myself today and nothing would
13   happen." Then, retching Saturday became Good-morning
14   Monday and I'd already made up my mind: I'm going to
15   look for a life in twenty-four hours, and if I don't find
16   anything, then I'll kill myself this very night and that's
17   that. It didn't take more than twelve hours. And it wasn't
18   just talk. At four P.M. I signed up for flight attendant
19   training. It wasn't a job, but at least it was an idea, the idea
20   of flying, by then I wasn't killing myself that night and
21   anyway, in my current condition, if the plane crashes, I
22   was already on the ground. If it hurtled toward earth, who
23   better than me to explain to the passengers the position to
24   assume when it's time for us to die, to feel like crash site
25   debris, to burn in flames when you're cut to bits? Who if
26   not me? Hmm? Besides, I saw a poster with the flight
27   attendant's uniform and I loved it. "As good as I look in
28   blue." Beautiful. Though my only problem is I'm terrified
29   of heights. A small thing, if you want to be a flight
30   attendant. Phobic me, terrified at any height. Me, with a
31   fear so intense, I feel it even working "ground crew," it
32   eats me up even walking in very high heels, because they
33   still make us wear heels, or else they screw you. And with
34   my fear of heights and everything, I took the course and
35   they liked me and I liked it. I became a star pupil,

1   everyone knew my full name, which with everything else
2   I didn't know myself until then. I didn't want to kill myself
3   and that was progress. I think. Right? In a year I was
4   already Cockpit Attendant on domestic flights. And in
5   eighteen months they gave me my first international
6   flight. Until a couple months ago I started feeling
7   symptoms of my illness again, the same one airline
8   doctors diagnosed me with yesterday, the same one I
9   talked to my anal flight chief about this morning, when
10 she said with this illness on my shoulders, this would be
11 my last flight, my last flight through the heavens. Because
12 of this illness that doesn't keep me from working, but it's
13 not acceptable to the company, because I'm a danger.
14 Here, where they save on fuel and we all fly with that gun
15 to our heads. Here, where they cut back on turbine
16 maintenance checks to save dough. Here, where they
17 don't check the runway, don't inspect the landing gear,
18 don't change the tires 'til they blow; here where they give
19 away tickets to their friends without asking for ID,
20 without checking them, without reminding them that it's
21 better to be polite than an animal. Here, in this world, I'm
22 the danger. Because of my illness. And even though I can
23 control it with medication, they've said flying, flying no.

Communicating through the Sunset
by Kerri Kochanski

Rachel – 16   **Serious**

The following piece challenges the actress to touch bottom with her deepest fears and most unsettling personal feelings of revulsion. Rachel has been raped: first as a young girl of seven and now as a teenager, and she has stabbed the abusive young man to death in order to protect herself. As she speaks to her friend, Frankie (who has just pathetically admitted to her that once he ate some pet tadpoles), Rachel must deal with the turbulent feelings that have arisen as a result of her experiences. She is unable to speak to her mother now, nor to her stepfather, Jimmy. The monolog requires high energy throughout, taking the listener on a journey through semi-rational explanations, explosive outbursts, nightmarish memories, reflective pauses, and desperate struggles in order to make sense of all that has happened to her. Particular care must be taken with pacing the speech, and the author has suggested key points where pauses should interrupt the flow of words. Yet despite the semi-incoherence of Rachel's thoughts and words, there is a strong sense of development here, and Rachel discovers in the end a comforting degree of self-reliance from all she has learned.

1 RACHEL: Well, it's not like I went and fried up some tadpoles,
2   Frankie. I mean, I *killed* somebody. Not just somebody. My
3   *step*brother. *(Pause. She begins to grow uncomfortable.*
4   *Decides to continue.)* It's the way Jimmy looks at me when
5   I say I'm sorry ... And my mom: "Things like this happen to
6   girls ... Things like this happen to girls all the time ..." *(She*
7   *begins to let it rip.)* It just wasn't gonna be like those other
8   times ... Not when I was *innocent* and *stupid* – and *seven*
9   *years old* – and didn't know enough until I read my books
10   and realized ... what Billy's doing to me ... ? It really is this
11   horrible thing I think, even though he says ... *(Pause,*

1   *regains control of herself.)* **See, when Dad died ...** *(Pause.)* **He**
2   **gave us food! Clothes! A place to live! Jimmy?!? He'd kick**
3   **us out ... and it would be back to the library ... or the woods**
4   **... And it wasn't all bad, Frankie. Not all the time ... But**
5   **sometimes ... like last ...** *(She suddenly cries out.)* **Where is**
6   **that man on the other side of the sunset?! I want to ask**
7   **him – if his stepbrother was raping** *him* **– if he was so fat**
8   **he couldn't even feel it, until he finally rolled off – 'cause**
9   **I was crazy ... screaming at the world ... crying at the sky ...**
10   **praying to heaven ... wishing for some angel to fly down –**
11   **fly down to explain to me this thing I'd done ...** *(Pause.*
12   *Mystified)* **Where'd the knife come from ... ? What had I**
13   **done ... If no one would help ...** *(She trails off. Becomes*
14   *resigned to what she has done.)*

Kara in Black
by Max Bush

Rachel – 19   **Serious**

In this speech, Rachel (who is Jewish) faces a group of women of varying ages who are staging a silent protest, all dressed in black, against the Iraq war. Her friend, Kara, to whom she speaks here occasionally, has a sister, Della, who is Rachel's best friend and a soldier in Iraq. Rachel also directs part of her speech at one of the teachers who is supporting the female students in their protest. The monolog challenges the actress to sustain a high level of intensity throughout without allowing the entire speech to become strident and over the top. In fact, there are one or two points where the playwright suggests that Rachel pull back and speak more quietly without losing her intensity. The fact that the crowd of women protestors never say a word (Women in Black) can add to Rachel's frustration and help drive the speech forward. The speech can be presented with a few pieces of paper that can indicate the photographs of atrocities that Rachel has brought with her; and the actress can deliver all of it directly to the audience, as though facing the crowd of silent young women whom she's addressing. See also other monologs from this play included in this section of monologs for women and in the section of monologs for men.

1   **RACHEL: How can you call yourselves women of peace when**
2   **you support the Palestinians? The terrorists who blow up**
3   **innocent women and children? There's blood on your**
4   **hands, now. There can be no peace until the bombings**
5   **stop! Do you even know who Hamas is? What the al-Aksa**
6   **Brigade does? Before nine-eleven Hamas had killed more**
7   **Americans than any other terrorist organization. Did you**
8   **know that? Look!** *(RACHEL holds up a picture of a bloody*
9   *child. Then she lays it at the feet of the women.)* **This is what**
10   **you are supporting! Look!** *Look!* **You want us to look at**

1   your pictures! You look, too! *(To Ms. Furman)* You — you
2   know who Hamas is and you know what they do and
3   you're out here dressed in their clothes?! You're betraying
4   your own people! Does your family know about this? Is
5   that why they're not here? And you forget — we cannot
6   forget — that Saddam financed suicide bombers in Israel
7   — he attacked Israel in the Gulf War — and you're trying to
8   stop   us   from   destroying   him?   Where   is   your
9   understanding? Your loyalty to our people? You're a
10 teacher! What are you teaching your students?! *(To another*
11 *fellow student who is protesting)* And you, you should be
12 waving the flag for your sister, Della. She's fighting a
13 noble war against a vicious enemy. An enemy of all
14 humanity. Look what he did to his own people — his own
15 people! *(RACHEL holds up pictures of dead Kurds, women*
16 *and children.)* He gassed them — women and children. He
17 killed thousands! Look! *(Holding up pictures)* First the gas
18 burned through their throats, then they vomited — Look!
19 — then they went blind, then their faces turned black and
20 they died. What would he do to us if he had the chance?!
21 Your sister is over there fighting these monsters and this
22 is how you respect her? There can be no peace until the
23 killers are destroyed. Della knows that! Why don't you?
24 *(Much quieter, though no less intense)* Because you are
25 ignorant. You are all ignorant, and don't know what
26 you're doing, wearing your black clothes of death. *(She*
27 *lays down the rest of her pictures at their feet.)* They're
28 counting on you, you know. They're confident of your
29 indifference. Because of people like you, we ignored them
30 for   years,   even   after   Saddam   killed   hundreds   of
31 thousands of people. And we let him go on killing. But not
32 anymore. *(Loudly again)* Women and children are dying
33 because we haven't fought hard enough! We must fight,
34 women must fight, women-must-fight — or die with their
35 children!

Have Mercy
by Hope McIntyre

Louise — 20s   **Serious**

In the following monolog, Louise describes some details of the abuse she and her siblings experienced at the hands of her father while she was growing up, and explains why she's reluctant to testify against the man now, years later. But the piece is more than just a list of all-too-familiar horrors in a young girl's life. The monolog is also a journey of discovery because Louise comes to realize as she speaks that she, too, must assume some responsibility for what happened to her. She also realizes that perhaps her half-brothers and half-sisters — the offspring of her father's abuse against her sisters — might possibly be even worse off than she is. And her feelings now towards her mother are similarly ambivalent. More than simply anger and bitterness, therefore, the monolog also reveals self-doubt, pity, vulnerability, and shame. The actress must stay alert to this constantly-changing emotional palette, and must also find a strong vis-à-vis to whom Louise is presumably speaking — to one of her sisters? To her current husband? To a therapist or a law enforcement officer? The choice of listener, in fact, can add a great deal of energy to the speech. See also a scene from this play included in the section of scenes for two women.

1 LOUISE: He was a stuffed, hairy pig. All pink and fat. When he
2   got angry he'd turn bright red like a cherry. He was always
3   "the man" because I had no love for him. None of us did. I
4   was fifth of ten. I mostly stayed invisible. I was scared of
5   him, sure. When I was nine he tried to touch me and I took
6   a pitchfork and stuck him like the stuffed pig that he is. I
7   knew he'd try to kill me after that, so I run off. Never went
8   back, never want to go back, neither. There's too much
9   blackness there, and I don't think that'll ever change even
10   with him in prison. Everyone thought he was some evil

force, stronger than anything, unstoppable. But, he's a fat old man, and he's mortal. Now, the babies, well it's too bad about them. What would you do if you thought you'd given birth to the devil's spawn? Nancy never thought of them as babies. My mother figured that it was the least she could do for her. That's what happens when you feel you've got no options. I'd seen enough. He'd take one of my sisters off to the bushes and we all knew why. The boys, now them he'd just beat. Beat them somethin' fierce. It was the girls he saved the rest for, three outa the six of us on a regular basis. There was other babies, too, aside from those Ma killed. I saw Nancy after they'd arrested him and she was pregnant again. Seemed like she was constantly pregnant. I guess she was the most fertile of us all. Margaret only had the one baby before I left. Nah, I don't wanna testify. Can you imagine talking about all this in front of everyone? It's not that I don't love my Ma, but ... well ... none of us was close. We was too worried about surviving, trying to stay invisible, and sometimes that meant wanting him to notice someone else. So, in that way, I guess we're all guilty.

Vamp
by Ry Herman

Angela – 20s   **Seriocomic**

One of the strengths of the following selection is that it allows the actress to speak directly to the audience at all points; and even though it may seem like a lecture, it turns very personal about midway through the dramatic action. The monolog's conclusion presents several key choices for the actress to make with regard to the overall interpretation: is Angela hilariously going off the deep end? Or does she become tragically entrapped by her own personal experience and lose her initial train of thought? Does she begin the presentation comically and satirically and suddenly discover at some point that her amusing remarks are more profound than she at first imagined? The monolog is complete as it stands, although it may be shortened for certain purposes without losing a great deal of its unique appeal. When staged as a studio exercise, the actress may choose to employ the stage props indicated (easel and placards), but the piece can also be presented effectively without any props at all.

1   *(An easel stands beside ANGELA, holding a number of*
2   *placards. The text on the first placard reads "VAMPIRES,"*
3   *with an appropriate picture.)*
4   **ANGELA: Ummmm … hi. I was … uh … thinking it might be a**
5   **good idea right now to have a little talk about vampires.**
6   **Vampires seem to be pretty much everywhere these days,**
7   **right? I mean, they're in books, they're in films, they're on**
8   **TV – and so most people probably think they have a pretty**
9   **good handle on what vampires are all about. But actually,**
10 **there's a lot of misinformation out there, and a lot of big**
11 **gaps in what "everybody knows." Let's take the television,**
12 **OK? I mean, nearly every vampire you see on TV is the**
13 **European Dracula type. Think about it, when was the last**

1   time you saw an Asian hopping vampire or an African
2   mumiani on a show? It's like they don't even exist. *(She*
3   *removes the first placard to reveal the second one that*
4   *depicts vampires of all ethnicities.)* **And the U.S. Census still**
5   **doesn't even have a "vampire" category, so nobody even**
6   **really knows exactly how many there are. And it's not easy**
7   **to estimate, because it's almost impossible to tell the**
8   **difference between a town with vampires and a town**
9   **where people just happen to bite each other a lot. What**
10   **I'm trying to say is, most people really know a lot less**
11   **about vampires than they think they do. So, I'd like to**
12   **start by dispelling a few common vampire myths.** *(She*
13   *reveals the third placard that reads "Myth Number One:*
14   *everyone a vampire bites becomes a vampire," with an*
15   *appropriate picture.)* **Myth Number One: everyone a**
16   **vampire bites becomes a vampire. This is a totally**
17   **ridiculous idea. I mean, just do the math. Say you start**
18   **with just one vampire. Even if vampires only bit someone**
19   **once a month, that means everyone in the world would be**
20   **a vampire in under three years.** *(She reveals the fourth*
21   *placard that reads "$2^{33} = 8,589,934,592$," with pictures of lots*
22   *and lots of vampires.)* **Actually, turning people into**
23   **vampires is, trust me, a long and complicated procedure.**
24   **Which is why, instead of being surrounded by vampires**
25   **right now, you're surrounded by werewolves.** *(She reveals*
26   *the fifth placard that reads "Myth Number Two: vampires*
27   *kill their victims," with an appropriate picture.)* **Myth**
28   **Number Two: vampires kill their victims. This one**
29   **probably does more damage to the reputation of vampires**
30   **than anything else. I mean, if you're prejudiced, this is**
31   **probably why, right? But it's just crazy. Where are the**
32   **reports of morgues filled with bloodless corpses with**
33   **neck hickeys? Actually, vampires don't have to kill anyone**
34   **at all, necessarily. You see, there's only so much a vampire**
35   **can drink at a time, and it's just not enough to do real**

1   damage. They're actually sort of like vegetarians, except
2   they don't even kill vegetables. *(She reveals the sixth*
3   *placard that reads "Myth Number Three: all vampires suck*
4   *blood," with appropriate picture.)* **Myth Number Three: all**
5   **vampires suck blood. In fact, vampires feed in all kinds of**
6   **different ways. Some of them, for example, can use**
7   **practically any bodily fluid at all. But, let's not go there.**
8   **There are other vampires that are actually allergic to**
9   **blood, and have to make do with a variety of soy-based**
10   **blood substitutes. And some don't feed on anything even**
11   **resembling blood. That kind usually starts out by telling**
12   **you that they love you. And when they do, things can**
13   **really be great, at first, anyway. They're exciting, they're**
14   **fun, and maybe they've got a few problems, but you're**
15   **pretty sure you can deal with it, because they love you,**
16   **right? But after awhile, things start to go wrong. They get**
17   **kind of cold, or they get angry for no reason. But you**
18   **figure, hey, every relationship has problems, right? So you**
19   **try to talk it out, make everything happy again. But it**
20   **doesn't work. They get angry with you for bringing it up at**
21   **all. They say you're making the problem worse. Or that**
22   **you're the one creating the problem by talking about it. So**
23   **after awhile, you learn not to bring up anything bad. Not**
24   **to accuse them of anything. Just smile and stay happy and**
25   **maybe things won't get any better, but at least they won't**
26   **get any worse. But things do get worse. You don't know**
27   **why. Everything's going wrong, and somehow it's your**
28   **fault. You're not doing it right. You're not loving enough.**
29   **If you loved them enough, everything would be fine, but**
30   **it's not so you need to love them more and more, but it**
31   **never seems to be enough, and it goes on and on, and you**
32   **just think, what's wrong with me? It isn't her fault, she**
33   **told me what I'm not supposed to say, and what I'm not**
34   **supposed to do, but I just keep screwing up. And then one**
35   **day, when she slaps you, nothing unusual, not even a hard**

1   slap, but you just start ... screaming and screaming and
2   kicking and biting and that was it, it was over, and it was
3   all my fault, because if I had loved her enough, everything
4   would have been all right, but I couldn't, I didn't have it in
5   me, I couldn't love her enough, because I'm bad, I'm a
6   bad, mean person and I can't really love anybody, I can't ...
7   I can't ...

The Gifted Program
by Ruben Carbajal

Cyndi – 17   **Serious**

Cyndi is speaking in the high school corridor with Paul after reading his love letter to her. Paul is generally regarded by his schoolmates as a nerd, while Cyndi is a good-looking and popular blond cheerleader. Paul has also been crippled since he was a young boy, and now he wears braces and walks with difficulty. The monolog challenges the actress in several ways, most importantly by its tone of sincerity: Cyndi has probably never admitted to anyone before what she's telling Paul about her fears, insecurities, and shortcomings. In fact, the actress might choose to express these ideas not as something she's always known about herself but instead as self-discoveries she makes while trying to speak very honestly to her admirer. A second important challenge for the actress here is to express Cyndi's terrible self-conflict. She's profoundly touched by Paul's letter, and fully realizes that her present boyfriend, athletic Phil, lacks all the inner qualities that Paul possesses. Yet she can't dump Phil for Paul because she enjoys sharing in Phil's external success and wild popularity. And she despises herself for this. The playwright describes her as possessing "a slight sliver of self-consciousness that few can detect." Students may also want to read Paul's monolog to Cyndi in the monologs for men section of this collection.

1   **CYNDI: Your friend Steve gave me this.** *(She produces a letter.)*
2   **This ... this is beautiful. It's the most beautiful thing I've**
3   **ever read ... your handwriting is really hard to read, but**
4   **the words ... the words ... they made me cry. Wait. Please. I**
5   **want to get this out ... please? I don't know what you see in**
6   **me. I really don't. I think I know you better than you know**
7   **me.** *(Beat.)* **I know what it's like to be ignored.** *(Beat.)* **A**
8   **year-and-a-half ago, no one in this school knew who I was.**
9   **For the longest time I didn't have any friends. I wondered**

1   what was wrong with me. I saw all the popular kids and I

2   wondered what they had, how they did it. I just didn't get

3   it, you know? Then, my body changed. It was the weirdest

4   thing. It was like suddenly, I was visible. People started

5   treating me differently. I could feel the weight of people

6   staring at me. I started getting phone calls. Boys. I was

7   asked to try out for cheerleading. My tryout stunk. They

8   still let me in. All those people I secretly hated for so long

9   were now my friends. And not because my personality was

10   especially great, or I was smart or funny or talented ... For

11   no other reason other than the fact I had this body. I

12   thought I was different. I always secretly thought I was so

13   different from them. *(Shifts her tone.)* I'm so damned

14   angry at you, Paul, for what you've done. *I'm not any*

15   *different, do you understand?* *(Quieter)* I can't return

16   these feelings for you, even though I know inside that

17   you're probably the most beautiful person in this school. I

18   can't see past the *outside* of you. I just can't. I don't

19   deserve words like this, Paul. I'm not the person you think

20   I am ... Phil couldn't in a million years express himself the

21   way you do ... He's too in love with himself ... he's too

22   stupid. But I can't give him up for you. There's no way. I'm

23   just not brave enough, Paul. You're so sweet and smart

24   and kind. Some lucky person is going to realize that, Paul.

25   But it's just not me. *(Beat.)* I'm sorry, Paul. I'm so sorry.

American Midget
by Jonathan Yukich

Girl – Teens to 20s   Seriocomic

In the following selection, the young woman is responding to the first-hand discovery of her father's suicide. The monolog challenges the actress to provoke a grotesque response of black humor by presenting the ear-cutting example in an ambiguous fashion: does such a doctor exist, or is the Girl making this up? Should we laugh or cry; is the example real or over-the-top? The monolog also has a strong narrative quality with a clear beginning-middle-end structure that the actress must play because it can add great dynamism to the enactment and bring the piece to a solid finish. As the Girl tells her story, the actress will find a range of emotional colors along the way: sarcasm, guilt, pathos, incredibility, and self-certainty, among others.

1   GIRL: After father died, I became obsessed with hospitals. I'd
2   cut school and go daily. Pad and pencil in hand, incognito,
3   I surveyed how doctors would inform family members
4   that their loved ones had passed on. I became an expert.
5   Some doctors are cold and remote – in with the news and
6   quickly out before the messy freefall. Others sent their
7   nurses to do the deed. Many of the older types recite the
8   same tired script they've processed through the years. The
9   younger tend to be more expressive, beating back the
10   tears in a hammed-up display of compassion. There's one
11   doctor, however, an old woman of many wrinkles, who
12   simply looks into their gloomy faces and pauses. And just
13   stares. Empty, like a robot. And the loved ones crumple to
14   the floor, heaving and wailing at the loss of a parent, a
15   spouse, or a child. And this woman of many wrinkles does
16   not bend to assist or hearten. Instead, she removes a razor
17   from her pocket and adeptly slices off one of their ears.

1   The injured recoil with astonishment, blood spilling from
2   their flesh, as the doctor calmly walks away, returning
3   razor to pocket. Then, the best part. After the initial
4   shock, the wounded scream with the suffering of losing
5   an ear or a loved one. It's hard to tell which. Wallowing in
6   bloody tears, ache overtaking grief, grief overtaking ache,
7   the pain comes to the surface in a cathartic soft shoe for
8   the ages. Intense stuff. Far cooler than boy bands or
9   cheerleading practice, you can be sure of that. I never
10   understood how the doctor could get away with it, or why
11   she'd do such a thing to begin with. But what puzzles me
12   most is why the wounded, a month or two later, always
13   find the old woman of many wrinkles to express their
14   sincerest thanks. And, in return, she gives back their ears.

Friends Like These
by Melissa Dylan

Nathalie — 20s-30s   **Comic**

This monolog moves dynamically and relentlessly from quiet struggle to outright hysteria, as Nathalie tries to distinguish sanity from insanity. There is only one issue here — to get a grip! — and the actress should carefully pattern her rising hysteria from start to finish (with the help of the playwright's suggestions), as she wrestles throughout with her rising sense of panic. Space is also important here, since the locale is a restaurant or diner; thus Nathalie could play the situation as very public with other customers listening, or as private with only herself and Dave in the restaurant. The locale can also suggest business to the actress who may see herself bustling about the tables or the counter and fussing with odds and ends. Dave isn't completely loopy. Even though he has just told her that his imaginary friends (to whom Nathalie has been serving actual dinners for years) hate his guts, and he asks her what she thinks he should say to them. In the original play, neither Nathalie nor Dave realized that his dinner guests were imaginary!

1 NATHALIE: Look, Dave, you need to understand something.
2 You have come in here by yourself for years now — I don't
3 know how many. And at first I thought it was a joke, you
4 asking me to take orders from four people who aren't
5 there. So I played along — I have a sense of humor too,
6 right? But it happened again. And again. And again. *(Her*
7 *speech grows more frenzied.)* It happened, in fact, every
8 Wednesday for as long as I've worked here — which, we
9 both know, has been far too long. Every Wednesday
10 afternoon, I open the restaurant, and your ... uh ... group ...
11 is the first one here. Before any other customers, or even
12 my manager, you're here. I bring out five drinks. Five

1 entrées. And I set them all on the table, and then you talk
2 to yourself. All through dinner you sit there alone and you
3 talk, and you complain, and you sometimes laugh, and
4 there is *no one there* talking or laughing with you! *(She is*
5 *nearing hysteria.)* So I think ... OK! This guy is a nut job, but
6 I can handle it. After all, you're a regular customer, you
7 always pay for five meals, and Goddammit — *you tip really*
8 *well*! So I ignored the fact that while you seem like a
9 relatively normal guy, you have four imaginary friends
10 with you wherever you go! I mean, it did seem crazy, but
11 not *that* crazy! *(Hysteria hits.)* But today. Today! *Today I*
12 *find out that your imaginary friends hate you, and that is*
13 *more than I can handle any more!*

Foreign Bodies
by Susan Yankowitz

Sarah — 16   Serious

This monolog moves directly and relentlessly from beginning to end, and challenges the actress to carefully plot her emotional development so the climax isn't reached too early. In fact, Sarah has two or three other smaller climactic points as she develops her tirade, and the actress should choose these so that all create a pattern that leads her to her final conclusion and accusation. Along the way of this development, there are a range of emotional colors and structural turns that it's important to play: the frequent rhetorical questions, the explosions of outrage, the sarcasm, the incredulity, etc. The monolog could occur anywhere, and this gives the actress a choice of different locales that might help the dramatic action: in a car while driving? Over the family dinner table? While Dad is watching TV or relaxing at home? As he's going out the door to work? Above all, however, the speech becomes most compelling when the actress can express how much of Sarah's love for her father has been shattered by his recent behavior.

1   SARAH: How can you do it, Dad, how can you justify it? I'm so
2   ashamed I could die. My own father taking sides with a
3   sickie like that, my own father! And you never told me!
4   Sure, people have to get defended, sure they have their
5   constitutional rights, but you don't have to be the one, you
6   don't have to defend a scumbag who cuts women into
7   pieces and dumps them in the river! How would you feel
8   if it's because of you he gets off and into the streets again?
9   How do you know I won't be the next one he grabs?
10 Because it could be anyone, me or Kate or even Mom —
11 even Mom. One was a teenager, just like me. You know
12 that and you don't care. You just want to have your name

1   in the paper, you want to be on the news. Well, I saw your
2   name in the paper today and all my friends saw it, too, and
3   they think there's something wrong with you, they think
4   it's disgusting you're defending him. And so do I. You're
5   going to sit in the same room with that guy day after day,
6   for months, maybe, and don't you think it rubs off on you,
7   the way he thinks, the way he feels, don't you think it will
8   infect you? Well, it will, it will, you can't escape it, you'll
9   come home at night, and you'll kiss me and smell of him,
10 and of lies and blood and his filthy hands on those poor
11 women, those poor women reeled out of the river stinking
12 like fish, and you're bringing that into my home and
13 Mom's home, and you're my father. My father! How can
14 you look at yourself in the mirror? How? I can't look at
15 you! I'll never be able to look at you again!

Wait Wait Bo Bait
by Lindsay Price

Tamara — Teens–20s   **Comic**

This monolog is taken from a play about all the different ways in which people wait. The surface meaning of the monolog is self-explanatory, so the actress can focus more upon what's going on with Tamara between the lines — the subtext. And this offers the actress many choices. Is she angry? Slightly loopy after waiting so long for her call? Desperate and pleading? Puzzled and hurt? All of the above at different points? The piece also challenges the actress to play believably to an inanimate object (the telephone) and an imaginary audience (the Vegas crowd), eliciting some charming humor as she does so. And don't overlook the different ways of interpreting the last line, which can spin the interpretation rather differently and surprisingly at the very end.

1 **TAMARA:** *(Singing by making up the melody)* **Oh, Mister Phone.**
2 **Why don't you ring? Why don't I hear you sing in the**
3 **night? Oh, Mister Phone. One ding-a-ling is all I need to**
4 **make it right.** *(Speaking as if to a Vegas audience)* **Thank**
5 **you. Thank you very much. I'm here all week. You know,**
6 **just before I go, I'd like to send out a little word. Just a**
7 **little word out there to all the guys in the world.** *(Singing)*
8 **To all the guys in the world. If you meet that special girl.**
9 **Don't make her wait by the phone. All alone. 'Cause that's**
10 **not nice. She might curse you and wish that you had lice.**
11 **How'd you like that? Have to shave your head and buy a**
12 **hat.** *(Speaking)* **Thank you. Thank you very much. Try the**
13 **buffet. All you guys out there in the world. Could you do us**
14 **gals a favor? It's just a simple, teeny, tiny little thing. If you**
15 **don't want to call a girl then don't ask for her number.**
16 **Sounds easy, don't you think, audience? Don't ask for her**

number. Don't look her in the eyes and say, "I'm going to call you." Don't say it. Don't say those five little words. Would that be so hard? I don't think so. "I'm going to call you." Five little words that make girls all over the world cancel their plans and sit in their rooms going absolutely mental waiting for stupid boys to call. I know my life would be a lot better off if I had never heard them, isn't that right, audience? Ah, you're a beautiful crowd. *(Singing)* For centuries girls have waited for that invitation to the ball. 'Cause a stupid boy has told her — "I'm going to call." For centuries girls have believed but over and over and over and over and over and over and over and over again we've been deceived. When will we learn? When will we ever, ever, ever, ever, ever, ever learn? *(Speaking)* Thank you. Thank you very much. Tip your waitress! Our next act is Gammy Sam and his trained seal Jo-Jo. Jo-Jo can play "You Light Up My Life" on the castanets. Let's hear it for Jo-Jo!

Big Girl
by Andrew Biss

Peggy – 20s   Comic

*This frank monolog needs to be spoken by an actress who is
somewhat large, either in terms of her height or her weight. It offers
the actress an excellent opportunity to speak directly to the audience
as a confidante and establish a warm and charming relationship with
her listeners. Of particular importance here is the need for Peggy to
develop as she speaks, so her words do not seem to be canned or pre-
planned recitations but discoveries and decisions instead. Peggy
should be different at the end than at the beginning; she must learn
something along the way. A second challenge here is that Peggy's
words are also tinged with sadness, some regret, and also some
embarrassing self-honesty, and these colors should not be lost amid
all the other comedy that is working in the piece.*

1   PEGGY: I've always been big. I was born big. I was a big baby.
2   Still am in some respects. In fact, one of the earliest
3   memories I have is of my Aunt Nester staring down at me,
4   her thin lips contorted into a forced expression of
5   adoration, saying to my mother, "My word, you've got a big
6   girl there, haven't you, Georgie." *(Pause.)* She's dead now.
7   Not my Mother – my Aunt Nester. A severe stroke whilst
8   pruning her beloved roses in her front garden. She fell
9   into them face first, the thorns of her pride and joy
10   gashing open her wizened face in her moment of need.
11   They did a good job, though – at the mortuary, that is. She
12   looked quite regal, all dished-up and served before us,
13   there in her casket. I stared hard at her face, but I couldn't
14   see even the trace of a scar. Mum fell apart. Sadly, all I felt
15   was a slight twinge of guilt as I contorted my not-so-thin
16   lips into a forced expression of loss. *(Pause.)* And so it goes.

1   *(Pause.)* **I think self-hatred is vastly underrated, don't you?**
2   **I mean, everyone seems to have such a negative view of it.**
3   **But if you really think about it, it makes life so much**
4   **easier in so many ways. For a start, you don't have to**
5   **bother about giving yourself all those tiresome**
6   **confidence-building pep talks inside your head every time**
7   **you look in the mirror or step outside the front door. You**
8   **can simply hate what you see before you, shrug your**
9   **shoulders, and get on with your business. And if someone**
10   **insults you or shoots you a disdainful glance, it doesn't**
11   **sting or chip away at your delicately crafted shell of self-**
12   **confidence — it just lands harmlessly in that boggy pit of**
13   **everything you already despise anyway and fizzles out**
14   **with barely a flicker. You don't wrestle with it, you just**
15   **absorb it. It can save an awful lot of time in this fast-paced**
16   **world of ours. Think about it.** *(Pause.)* **Anyway, I have to go.**
17   **I have a date.** *(She turns to leave, then stops and looks back*
18   *over her shoulder with a wry smile.)* **Yes ... even me.**

Eponine
by Colorado Tolston

Eponine – 17   **Serious**

In Victor Hugo's classic novel Les Miserables, *Eponine is the beautiful young streetwalker who falls desperately in love with Marius, one of the student leaders of the revolution. In this updated version, the same young Eponine has learned to survive on the streets alone in a large city, and has sometimes made horrible mistakes in order to find her way. In this scene, she's explaining her past life to Marius at the beginning of their relationship, and her feelings are mixed between hesitation and boldness, regret and pride, curiosity and self-discovery. Above all, the actress must avoid playing the speech as a sad confessional of guilt, and instead must remind herself why she's speaking: to reveal the truth about herself to her lover in the desperate hope that he'll accept her despite her checkered past. Finally, in terms of staging, the scene offers an excellent opportunity for the actress to play directly to the audience where Marius is listening.*

1   **EPONINE: I wonder if that's true. As I said, I walked all over**
2   **New York. I slept wherever I could, and you'd be surprised**
3   **at the places I found. I've always managed to find**
4   **someplace. As for food ... Well, I'm sure you have a few**
5   **ideas about that. You don't need to tell me what they are, I**
6   **can guess. I stole. I learned to be a thief before anything**
7   **else, and my life was no better than my namesake's, I'm**
8   **sure. And do you know what? It was easy. Easy to slip my**
9   **hand into an unsuspecting pocket, easy to sneak an apple**
10   **or a piece of bread when no one was looking, easy to take**
11   **what wasn't mine, and easy not to care about doing it. I'm**
12   **not proud of it, but that skill fed me for many years. And I**
13   **was good enough where I hardly ever got caught. And**

1   that's the only rule I knew: not to get caught. No one ever
2   bothered to teach me anything else. If they had ... I said
3   that I've never had any friends, but maybe that's not quite
4   true. There was one man who I guess was a friend, though
5   I never really got the chance to know him very well. I was
6   in the Village one day when the owner of a restaurant saw
7   me. He saw that I was hungry and invited me in for
8   something to eat. When I was finished he told me to come
9   back the next day, and I did. For two weeks he let me eat
10   until I was full and then told me to come back tomorrow.
11   Then one night someone I knew, not a friend, asked me to
12   crawl through one of the restaurant's back windows and
13   let him in. He didn't tell me why, and for the money he
14   offered I didn't ask. The next day I didn't go near the
15   restaurant for fear of the cops surrounding it. The day
16   after that I came back to find the restaurant closed,
17   bankrupt. The owner lost his life savings that night
18   because of me. *(She fights back tears.)* I had betrayed the
19   only person who had ever been anything like a friend to
20   me, and I didn't even know his name. I never saw that
21   man again. I don't know where he is now, but I hope he
22   can forgive me. I've done a lot of awful things in my life,
23   but nothing worse than that. I think that was the day that
24   I finally realized what my life really was. When I found
25   out that the restaurant was closed, I went somewhere to
26   hide and just cried. All I could do was cry. *(She wipes away*
27   *some of her tears and looks away.)* After what happened at
28   the restaurant I felt like reality had hit me in the face for
29   the first time. I couldn't eat or sleep for days, just cry and
30   cry and cry. I cried the tears of a lifetime. I felt so alone. I
31   suddenly realized how cut off I was from the rest of the
32   world and how that was the last thing I wanted. I wanted
33   so badly to be part of the world again! I didn't want to be
34   on the outside anymore. I wandered the streets, not
35   knowing or caring where I was going, until I finally

1   collapsed from exhaustion and hunger. That night I slept
2   at last and didn't wake up again until afternoon. When I
3   did, I could feel the sun warming me up, inside and out.
4   In the distance I heard the sounds of the city, but around
5   me there was only the whispering of the wind in the trees.
6   All was peaceful. I had come here. And here I didn't feel so
7   alone. I never have, I don't know why. I sat here the rest of
8   that day, not wanting to feel that awful emptiness again.
9   But by evening I got so hungry that I had to leave to find
10 something to eat. But knowing I had somewhere to come
11 back to made a difference. And something changed that
12 day. I could have easily stolen something like I usually did,
13 but I felt that that would have offended this peaceful
14 place. It sounds silly, I'm sure, but that's how I felt. So that
15 night I got my food honestly. It tasted so good, so clean,
16 just like the food at the restaurant. I wish I could say that
17 I never stole again, because I did. But it all felt different. I
18 learned that stealing pushed me further away from the
19 world while being honest brought me back to it. I got my
20 meals honestly whenever I could, which wasn't as often as
21 I wish. But it was a start, and I always had this place to
22 come back to. *(Pause.)* And that's my story, Monsieur
23 Marius. What do you think of me now?

Window of Opportunity
Roger Iverson

1 **Zinni – 20s-30s**   **Serious**

2

3 *This monolog challenges the actress to come to grips with the pain of*
4 *infertility that many young couples experience and to play those*
5 *feelings as sincerely and with as much belief as possible. Zinni is*
   trying to explain her need for children to her husband who really
6 *does not understand how empty she feels, how compelling the desire*
7 *for parenting can be for her, and her frustration as she desperately*
8 *compares her childless condition with others who seem to have no*
   regard for (and no difficulty with having) "a whole litter of kids." It
9 *also contains moments of private grief, of remembrance and regret,*
10 *of anger and determination. The structure is disarmingly simple as*
11 *Zinni's persuasiveness builds to a climax in the final lines; the actress*
12 *must play and experience each of Zinni's ideas fully, resisting the*
13 *temptation to rush to the finish.*

14

15 **ZINNI: Listen: if we don't have a child, we will forever be**
16   **childless. That's not a bump in the road, Albert. That's a**
17   **mountain range.** *(Pause.)* **Last Saturday I was sitting on the**
18   **corner at Starbucks watching people walk down Proctor**
19   **when a woman came by with her little girl. She was maybe**
20   **two. Her hair was blond silk and her cheeks were round …**
21   **I watched my hand, like it was someone else's, reach out**
22   **and caress her hair. Like touching nothing. Her mom**
23   **watched, smiling. Then she asked. Came right out and**
24   **asked me. She said, "Do you have a child of your own?"**
25   **What else could I say … ? "Yes," I lied. And she held open**
26   **the glass door for her daughter, and she smiled at me. And**
27   **for that moment I was that woman's equal. We were**
28   **colleagues. I was whole … I want to be whole, Albert. I**
29   **need to be a whole family. I would be such a beautiful**

1   mother. But I can't stand it any more, now. I hate being
2   alone. I hate the miscarriages. I hate my body! *I hate God!*
3   No! I want my baby! Some women who deserve nothing
4   have a whole litter of kids. From day one I've done
5   everything right. Waited for a husband. Waited for a
6   home. Waited for money. I take care of my body; eat fish
7   and prenatal vitamins every damned ... I devote my life to
8   teaching other people's kids ... I deserve! ... a child.

Kara in Black
by Max Bush

Furman – 25   **Serious**

Mrs. Furman is a young high school teacher who has been asked by some of her female students to serve as advisor for their newly formed group of Women in Black: women dressed all in black who stage silent protests in opposition to war and violence. As the speech makes clear, the issue of protest has forced Furman to deeply examine her own Jewish beliefs before announcing her decision to the students. Thus, the monolog is not a lecture, but a more personal and sincerely-felt public confession. In the original play, the speech is broken-up by comments from the students as Furman speaks, and some of that give-and-take interaction with the public can still be played here in the monolog. The actress can speak the piece boldly and directly to the audience, but should also try to express Furman's emotional indecision and self-conflict. Indeed, the speech may perhaps best be played as though Furman were opposed to the group when she begins to speak, but convinces herself of the opposite by the time she finishes. See also other monologs from this play included in this section of monologs for women and in the section of monologs for men.

1   FURMAN: I've had an interesting couple of days, thinking
2   about your presentation and about my own sense of this
3   war. I talked with my family, because as a Jew I wanted to
4   be clear about my decision. As I told you, if you had
5   decided on any other group – and there are other groups
6   I could tell you about – I wouldn't have a problem. *(Pause.)*
7   I understand you chose Women in Black because it was
8   nonviolent and protested violence toward *all* women and
9   children. I hate the suicide bombings in Israel, but I also
10   think I understand why they happen. The oppressive
11   policies of the Israeli government aren't bringing security

1   or safety or an end to violence. And the suicide bombings
2   aren't stopping the Israelis. Both forms of violence
3   continue the other. And I was thinking: Am I a Jew first
4   and a woman of the world second? Or am I a woman first
5   and a Jew second? Because I remembered my
6   grandmother talking about *tikkun olam* which I think
7   means "healing the world." That seems even more
8   important now. So, I've decided I'm a woman first and a
9   Jew second, and I see mothers and children dying and
10   grieving on both sides in Israel. And in Iraq and in
11   America. And I'm afraid if we invade Iraq we'll be
12   occupying their country and the same kind of situation
13   will happen as in Israel. So, I went to the principal and
14   asked if I could sponsor you. But our principal will not
15   allow us to have these meetings on the high school
16   campus. He doesn't think it's appropriate for the school to
17   sponsor you. He said he'd sponsor you if you were
18   interested in something about the Vietnam War, or the
19   Korean War, or World War Two – even the First Gulf War.
20   But he thought this would show a lack of support for the
21   troops. And their families. And he said he doesn't want to
22   divide the school. Or help divide the community. And,
23   frankly, he thought it would be unpatriotic. And then he
24   said: "Off the record. I have to live in this community."
25   *(Pause.)* So, if you think it's a good idea, we could hold the
26   meetings at my house.

Monologs
for Men

Harvest

by Diane Lefer

Cody – 17   Serious

The following monolog is extremely challenging to play effectively.
Cody is speaking to an attractive girl that he's just met about his
abusive stepfather, Duane, and his life with Duane on a Texas ranch
before they moved away. The speech contains a range of emotions
because Cody's feelings towards Duane are tangled and complex. He
certainly resents the abuse he's been receiving from his stepfather,
but he loves and sympathizes with Duane's situation, and has been
making a real effort to understand why Duane has been picking on
him since they left the Texas ranch. None of these feelings should be
lost or glossed over in the enactment. At the same time that Cody
wishes to share these feelings and experiences with Suzy, he is also
concerned about making a good impression on her. Thus, the context
of the monolog is further complicated by Suzy as the listener, and the
actor should decide which is the major thread here: Cody's
relationship with Duane or his growing relationship with Suzy. The
entire piece should take three to five minutes to perform and
shouldn't be rushed; but an actor might find it challenging to edit the
monolog to a shorter version for audition purposes.

1   CODY: If we could go back to Texas, Duane and I got along there. He
2   was happy, but he wasn't happy – it wasn't his land. We
3   worked for Mr. McGuire. Or Duane did. I was real young and
4   it took more strength'n I had, digging fence holes, stretching
5   bobwire. You see how hard Duane works, you can't help but
6   admire. Back then, he didn't hate me so much. He hated the
7   cows. Think that's strange? I thought you noticed. Duane can
8   hate anything he puts his mind to. But the fact about cows,
9   cows can go right through bobwire and not even graze their
10   hides. But they're so dumb, you put up the fence and they
11   don't even try to get through. You just let 'em know where you

1   draw the line and then they stay where you want 'em. Duane

2   hated them, and all they did was obey. That's when I figured

3   Duane would like you better if you defied him a little. I liked

4   it in Texas. We had horses and everything. Of course they

5   weren't ours. I wish I could take you there to see it. See, Suzy,

6   everything about the West has changed. You don't have cattle

7   drives up the old Chisholm Trail. You got ranchers with

8   airplanes and feed lots where they give cows shredded phone

9   books to eat. Everything's changed — except the cowboy. You

10   still got to rope 'em and castrate 'em — excuse me — by hand

11   the way it's always been done. Farming's not the same. No way

12   Duane can make it these days. Everything in the whole world

13   has changed. But for the cowboy. Everything. Except the

14   cowboy. Everything but. Am I talking too much? Back there at

15   the McGuire place, Duane, he knew how to do everything. Mr.

16   McGuire, he had this really brushy land, and Duane set up a

17   deer blind. Picked just the right place. One day, we're in the

18   pasture, me and Duane and Mr. McGuire, and a doe came

19   crashing out of the brush. Duane's on horseback and he's got

20   a lariat on the saddle. Roping a wild animal? A doe? I'm not

21   sure in the history of the world it had ever been done. But

22   Duane takes off racin' that horse and swingin' that rope — just

23   spinnin' it in the air — he throws it, and he's got her. Me and

24   Mr. McGuire, we could hardly believe it even though we seen

25   it. The doe starts kicking on the ground. Then she freezes and

26   holds still. Duane jumps off the horse and goes over to her and

27   he takes out his knife. He's got his knife in his hand. Duane,

28   he always keeps a sharp knife. He brings that blade to her

29   throat. And all of a sudden — pfft! He cuts the rope. Were the

30   rope he cut! She kicks, he jerks his head out of the way, and

31   she's gone. Duane didn't always take pleasure in giving out

32   hurt. *(Pause.)* Those were good times, Suzy, nothing ever went

33   wrong. I respected him then. You think he's angry because I

34   don't respect him now?

A Different Place
by Robin Graham

Abel — 20s   **Romantic**

*Abel is an immigrant seeking political asylum who has fallen in love
with Janie, a meditation teacher. His feelings of alienation in this
foreign land have mingled with his affection for Janie who seems to
have taken him under her wing and helped him to assimilate. In the
following extended monolog he recounts their recent separation at
the airport when she left to do missionary work. This extract from a
longer, one-actor monolog play is extremely challenging because the
entire context is reminiscence — something that is always dangerous
for the actor if he presents the events as something fixed in the past,
too calmly and unemotionally. Instead, the actor must strive to bring
the memory alive, to live it and experience it afresh as though it were
happening in the present. And even though Abel seems to be awash
in a sea of memories about Janie, his emotional development leads
clearly to the point at the end where he confesses to his absent vis-à-
vis that he loves her more than simply as a friend and teacher. There
are many discoveries here for the actor to play, as well as a sense of
urgency as Abel struggles to tell Janie in her absence what he could
not tell her when she was present.*

1   ABEL: Me and Janie under the cherry blossom tree. One month
2   ago. In Janie's garden. You see! It's in full blossom. Pink
3   against the blue of the sky. And beneath it is a carpet of
4   pink petals, and green where the grass and weeds point
5   through. And the dandelions and the daisies. Janie is next
6   to me. Isn't she slim! One inch waist! There's a cool breeze.
7   Birds that have been waking me up far too early every
8   morning have flown over to Janie's house and are still
9   chattering away, and Janie's cat is nowhere to be seen to
10   shut them up. It's the most beautiful day. I feel happy.
11   *(Pause.)* Until Janie is telling me that she is going away. Her

1   teacher has asked her to go away. To teach people how to
2   meditate. She has to go. Her teacher said. Her spiritual
3   teacher. He says in life we must do service to others. This
4   is her service. And she wants to go. Far away. She is taking
5   extended leave from work. She can let me stay in her
6   house while she's gone. But I don't want to. And I won't.
7   She'll telephone when she can, but it's very expensive.
8   And she'll be back before I know it. She says. And she says
9   I'll probably get up to all sorts of things when she's not
10 around. She says she thinks I'm a very special person, and
11 she'll think of me every day. I ask her, "Do you love me?"
12 Of course she does. She says. She loves everybody. But she
13 tells me I have to have a life of my own. And so does she.
14 *(Pause.)* A week ago. Barrier at the airport. She shows her
15 British passport. Janie can travel to any country in the
16 world. And she's off far away. To a land of ... giraffes.
17 Elephants. Parasols in the sun ... with a suitcase, half-
18 filled with suntan cream factor twenty-five, which she
19 bought last year when Boots the chemist had a special
20 offer, and she thought it would last her twenty-five years
21 so she bought so much because the offer was so good and
22 it's new, water resistant, easier to rub in, fragrance free, in
23 the green plastic bottle with a flip open cap, and I know as
24 she walked away that she didn't love me in the way I need
25 her to. She said, "Jai Guru Dev." She always says "Jai Guru
26 Dev." She looked into my eyes, and kissed my forehead.
27 Showed her passport. And disappeared off to the duty-
28 free shops before they disappear, too. "Peace be with you,
29 Janie. Look after yourself." She turned, waved at me,
30 laughed. "Ha-ha-ha." Disappeared round the corner. Then
31 popped her head back round. Waved at me. Laughed. And
32 disappeared. Three minutes later. I'm still at the barrier.
33 She popped her head round the corner again. She sees I'm
34 still there. She calls out, "I'm going now. Take good care of
35 yourself. Jai Guru Dev ..." *(Pause.)* Why? When I'm only just

getting to know you. I am so helpless. I want to push that barrier down. I can only watch, and smile, and show I am happy for you. And know that every night, and every day, I shall be dreaming of you. In my mind, as it's always been. I shall survey your face, touch your forehead, stroke my fingers in your greying hair. Look so deeply into your green speckled eyes that I shall see into your soul and right round the back of it. I shall see so clearly every crack in your makeup where the wrinkles are when you've smiled and giggled. I shall feel your breath, your kalamata olive and garlic breath. And hear your hiccups after you've eaten too quickly because you have work to do. I love you, Janie, until it hurts in my chest. And now you can just walk away. You have to love me. You have to love me how I want you to love me. Tell me what I can do. Because I am at the airport saying goodbye. The barrier stands between us. With security men checking documentation. Security men who keep me in my place. Yes. I have been here before. Seen real barriers that stop real people from living. Real torture, persecution, prejudice. Barriers that separate families and friends. Control the so-called undesirable. I have been here before ...

Cuthbert's Last Stand
by Andrew Biss

Cuthbert – 20s   **Comic**

Does any mother name her child Cuthbert any longer? Surely the title tips you off immediately about the comic tone of this monolog that deals with a young man trying to cut the apron strings of parental control. The comic lynchpin, however, is thoroughly modern: Cuthbert's mother is terrified her son is heterosexual. More than that, the monolog also implies that she has actually raised him to become a homosexual. This suggests the tone is not simply comical, but over-the-top farce. As with all farce, melodrama, or soap opera, the actor must avoid camping the enactment (playing it tongue-in-cheek). Instead, it challenges the actor to play it seriously with utmost belief, as though Cuthbert really were afraid of hurting his mother's tender feelings.

1   CUTHBERT: That's right, go ahead and laugh. Laugh away. Get
2   it all out of your system. Because when I'm finished what
3   I'm about to say, I doubt very much that laughter is going
4   to be among your top ten list of immediate responses.
5   *(With great difficulty)* You see, I ... I've no idea how many
6   times I've attempted to tell you this in the past ... and how
7   many times my courage has simply up and left me, but I ...
8   I can't maintain this façade any longer, Mother. I can't
9   continue with the lies ... the deceit ... the pretense. I can't
10   go on saying one thing and feeling another. You see, the
11   fact is, Mother, as hard as this is going to be for you to
12   accept ... or understand – especially when sober – the fact
13   remains ... the fact remains I am not the person you think
14   I am. The painful truth is ... *(Taking a deep breath)* I am not
15   ... and as far as I know, have never been ... a homosexual.
16   *(Pause.)* Well? Aren't you going to say something? Aren't

1   you going to tell me how ... disappointed you are? How I've

2   let you down? How ashamed you feel? *(Pause.)* I know this

3   has to be difficult to take in, but I ... I had to tell you. I

4   couldn't continue living this make-believe existence any

5   longer. *(Pause.)* And now that I have told you, I ... well, I feel

6   ... I feel wonderful, actually. And yet at the same time quite

7   dreadful. Dreadful because ... because I feel as though I've

8   just taken the entire image of everything that you thought

9   I was and smashed it into tiny pieces.

The Children's Teeth
by Nicolette Bethel

Ross — 30s   Comic

This straightforward monolog offers the actor an opportunity for storytelling at its best. It is a colorful, fast-building tale, filled with drama about an everyday incident on the road near Nassau, Bahamas. Ross is plainly pumped by his story — which has more than one point of excitement for the actor to play: the confusion of the cones on the road, the crushed pylons, the oncoming car, Ross's game of chicken, and the events following. The monolog also challenges the actor to master the Bahamian dialect for a distinctly original voice characterization of this wonderful character. Finally, there is ample opportunity for the actor to explore a range of physical actions and gestures to accompany the speech: acting-out the driving, responding physically to the emotional moments, reveling in the reactions of his listeners, and so forth.

1   ROSS: I tell you, bro, I swear, driving in this country getting
2   crazier and crazier. I tell you that. They get one pile a cone-
3   dem all down the airport road down there, seen, between
4   the lake and the airport. All them plastic orange cone jook
5   in the middle of the road, where the line is be. I'n know
6   what they doing. But the cone-dem right in the middle of
7   the road, all down. I say to myself, right now they'n want
8   nobody overtaking on this road, thas why they get these
9   cones in the middle here. So I driving along, looking at
10   these cone. Lil while, I start to see couple cone lying on
11   they side, this one mash up, this one roll this way, this one
12   roll that way, and I say to myself, right now you know
13   Bahamian people passing on this road anyhow. And sure
14   enough, just I coming down the hill past the lake — you
15   know, where the road curve and you could pick up speed

1   — just I coming out of the curve I see this nice new Lexus
2   coming towards me on my side of the road. He overtaking
3   three-four cars and now he stuck on my side cause bout
4   ten cone in the middle of the road over there, they'n been
5   knock down yet. So he looking for a space and he trying to
6   keep up he speed and keep ahead of the cars he was
7   passing and he trying to avoid me. Cause if there was a
8   crash you know who woulda win. So I speed up. I speed
9   up! I say to myself, all right dread, lessee who man now.
10   You want overtake, lessee who man. So I hit the gas and I
11   speed up. Boy. You shoulda seen him looking for a place to
12   get back on his side of the road! But you want know the
13   craziest thing? He get back on his side of the road and he'n
14   touch a cone. I look at him and I haddie say to myself,
15   that's some sweet driving, now. Some real handling. Not a
16   touch, not a scrape. I haddie stop the truck to go back and
17   look. And not a cone out of place. Man. If I ever meet him
18   again I haddie shake he hand. Fella could drive.

The Gifted Program
by Ruben Carbajal

Paul – 16   **Romantic**

*Paul is speaking in the high school corridor with Cyndi after she has
just read his love letter and told him that she can't love him. Paul is
generally regarded by his schoolmates as a nerd, while Cyndi is a
good-looking and popular blond cheerleader. Paul has also been
crippled since he was a young boy, and he now wears braces and
walks with difficulty. The monolog is built mainly upon Paul's need
to tell her in person how much he loves her, but it also contains other
intentions and emotional colors. For example, Cyndi has just
admitted to him that she can't get beyond the braces on his legs, and
she feels ashamed of that. So Paul is also trying to reassure her that he
really does know a lot about her and doesn't care about that. There
are other things, too, that Paul discovers as he speaks, which gives the
speech a spontaneous quality. Most important, the monolog
challenges the actor to express a great amount of sincerity in what he
says, and to capture the sense of cliff-hanging improvisation in this
deeply intimate moment with Cyndi. Students may also want to read
Cyndi's monolog to Paul in the monologs for women section of this
collection.*

1   **PAUL: Everyone I knew told me you'd never be able to care for**
2   **someone like me. I knew myself you probably couldn't.**
3   ***(Beat.)* But then I'd watch you. I see how you treat**
4   **everyone equally. I mean, I've never seen you be unkind to**
5   ***anyone*, no matter *who* they were. I see you, Cyndi, I've**
6   **watched you so closely for so long. Not a single thing that**
7   **you've done all year has escaped me. Every small detail**
8   **about you is so precious to me. I know that when someone**
9   **compliments you, you squint your eyes. Or that when**
10 **you're nervous, like right before a test, you push the same**
11 **strands of hair over your right ear. You like to bite the end**

1   of erasers, your favorite sweater is blue, when you're
2   bored in class you draw tiny flowers in the margins of
3   your notebook, until the whole page is filled with
4   scribbled daisies — but you know, the most obvious thing
5   about you, the thing that anyone who's known you for a
6   second can see, is that you're a good, a kind person ... I can
7   remember a time when I could run. I was really, really
8   small, like two or three ... I can remember running very
9   fast across our kitchen floor. My Dad says it never
10   happened. But I remember. I remember the feeling, it's so
11   vivid, you know? *(Beat.)* When I see you, when I talk to you,
12   when I close my eyes and *think* of you ... I feel like I'm
13   running. Nothing else in my entire life has ever come
14   close to giving me that sensation. *(Pause.)* I can't help how
15   I feel about you. I don't have a choice.

Suburban Redux
by Andrew Biss

Tristram – 20s   **Romantic**

Tristram is a shy, awkward young man who has just been rebuffed by the high-spirited woman whom he adores. He blames himself, but the actor must avoid self-pity here, as Tristram himself declares right at the outset. He understands and accepts his shyness and lack of creativity. Thus the monolog challenges the actor to struggle against his depression in two ways: by declaring his passionate adoration for his beloved and by taking pride in his own search for beauty and meaning in life. Does he really mean what he says to her? Or is he simply kidding himself and rationalizing his failure at love? In any case, for Tristram to simply beat himself up here in the monolog would be the kiss of death for an audience. We should see him struggling to find a way out of self-pity, even if he isn't entirely successful in the attempt.

1   TRISTRAM: No, no, it's quite alright. And it isn't self-pity, it-it's
2   self-knowledge. I'm quite aware of who I am. I'm quite
3   aware that I've never had a-a particularly interesting or
4   revealing thing to say or to contribute in my entire life.
5   And you needn't be kind, I-I'm not in need of sympathy.
6   Self-knowledge is a source of strength if one's able to
7   embrace it. But the fact remains, when you get right down
8   to it, I'm a decidedly dull individual, and it was stupid and
9   vain of me to imagine you could regard me as anything
10   else. But it's who I am. I don't wish to be dull. Who would?
11   I can imagine nothing more wonderful than to be an
12   object of fascination in the eyes of another. But no matter
13   how I try, it's not to be – not for me, at least. *(Pause.)* But,
14   you see, unlike your husband, whenever I look in the
15   mirror I'm more than capable of facing the truth –

1   however sobering. *(Pause.)* Oh, don't get me wrong — I-I'm
2   not saying I don't find *life* interesting. I do. I find it
3   immeasurably interesting, as I do people, and art, and
4   music, and literature ... and you. I think that must be why
5   I love you a-and love being with you as much as I do — you
6   fill in the bits of me that are missing. When I'm with you
7   I feel as though I *am* interesting and witty and clever. And
8   I'm sure any number of psychologists would be happy to
9   tell me that that's vicarious a-and weak and wrong of me,
10   but you see ... it makes me so very happy. *(Pause.)* But with
11   you, as with the arts, I'm simply a receptacle for someone
12   else's abilities. I absorb them, I feed on them, they enrich
13   me, but at the end of the day ... I bring nothing to the table.

Addiction
by Joel Murray

Elliot — 20s   **Serious**

Elliot is trying to win back the affections of his younger brother in this speech, which is filled with frustration, regret, hope, brotherly love, self-abuse, and wild promises. The speech allows the actor to draw upon his own imaginative and personal resources in order to build a background to the relationship between Elliot and his vis-à-vis; and to visualize how Elliot's brother is responding moment-by-moment to Elliot's words. Elliot is not just rambling on here in a drug-induced jag; it would be far more effective to play the speech as Elliot's struggle to shake off his drug habit once and for all since he knows what's at stake if he fails. In this regard, the language also poses a strong challenge: at times fragmented, at times insightful, at times desperate or even puzzled.

1 ELLIOT: I'm looking for a way to say I'm sorry. I mean, I stole a
2   lot of your life from you. I was supposed to be your big
3   brother, but I was ... the ... you know ... I couldn't let go of
4   the drugs, and then the drugs wouldn't let go of me. I ...
5   did things. Because of the drugs. I did so much terrible
6   stuff I can't ever take it back. *(Pause.)* Listen, remember,
7   remember when you were about five, Mom and Dad
8   bottomed out and got separated, so you started saving up
9   money ... ? *(Laughs.)* Yeah, you remember. Remember that?
10   You started saving up money to send them on a vacation
11   so they'd be happy and get back together. And, and ...
12   anyway, you had eight dollars saved up in this rusty
13   chicken soup can. You thought that'd get 'em to Venezuela
14   or some damn place. But you lost it, and Mom and Dad got
15   divorced, and you thought it was because you lost the
16   eight dollar vacation money. I was sick from seeing you

1   cry so hard. But ... see ... here's the thing. You didn't lose
2   the money. I stole it. *(Slight pause.)* I stole it and used it for
3   crystal meth. Ummmm ... This is going to seem so
4   meaningless, but — *(He pulls out a small roll of dollar bills.)*
5   Here's ... here's ... one, two, three, four, five, six, seven —
6   damn! *(He reaches back into his pocket and then checks all*
7   *his pockets.)* Seven. Where ... ? Where ... ? I had eight. I can't
8   believe this. I still ruin everything, don't I? No. OK. Look.
9   Look. All I'm trying to say is, from now on, I'll be there for
10   you. From here on out, I'm going to be your brother. You
11   don't have to believe me. I don't want you to believe me. I
12   want you to see for yourself, OK? OK. How about for
13   starters, you take the seven dollars. I'll get you eight. I'm
14   good for it.

Edible Shoes
by Jonathan Yukich

Garbanzo — 20s   **Comic**

The following piece demands a lot of enthusiasm on the actor's part because Garbanzo is absolutely ecstatic at what he's discovered. His best friend, Percy, tried to poison him some time ago, but as Garbanzo explains, Percy failed, and the poisoning simply enabled Garbanzo to take a long trip that has opened his eyes. For the first time in his life, his travels have impressed upon him the notion of the human community, and he feels rapturous in the knowledge. There are other emotional colors here, too: the wonderment over simple things, the curiosity about other people's daily living habits, the silly comedy that Garbanzo enjoys when pinching people. Although the monolog builds steadily to a climactic peak at the end, it challenges the actor to play it with absolute sincerity — which, of course, can be hugely amusing to the listener.

1   GARBANZO: Hey — it's no biggie. You don't have to apologize.
2   To tell you the truth, I haven't been home since you tried
3   to poison me with Ebola that day. I decided to see the
4   globe. You know, catch up on all that I had missed. I went
5   all over, Percy: Japan, the Mideast, Detroit. You would not
6   believe the stories that are out there. Seriously. Get this,
7   there are people, Percy, people in different clothes, in
8   remote lands, that live and breathe the same as you and I.
9   Yeah! I'm not joking. They eat and sleep, too. I mean, sure,
10   we read about them in books, you know, from a distance,
11   but I'm here to tell you *they are real*. I started pinching
12   them to be sure. They'd either yell something foreign, or
13   slap my face, but it didn't matter. You see, every yell, every
14   blow, confirmed that I — that *we* — are not alone. There are
15   so many stories, Percy! Each of them unique, desperate,

1   anonymous, but *real!* And I began to realize that there are

2   things in this world so glorious, so beautiful that I could

3   never attempt to express them in words. I can only collect

4   their images, sounds, and smells and love them for being

5   next to me.

Kara in Black
by Max Bush

Donovan — 18   **Romantic**

*Donovan delivers this prom invitation to Kara who is leading a silent
protest of women, all dressed in black, against the Iraq war. He's a
funny and spirited young man who does a program on a local radio
show, but who is sincere and cares for Kara. What makes this
monolog particularly challenging is that Donovan is speaking in
public, since Kara is surrounded by some of her silent female
classmates in the protest demonstration. Thus, Donovan (as he
admits at the beginning) should be having some amusing little fun at
the same time he's delivering an honest and tender invitation,
knowing that neither Kara nor her girlfriends can talk back to him! A
simple prop — Donovan's note — will suffice for playing the scene and
offer some possibilities for movement and gesture. Above all, the
actor must play the speech so compellingly that the listener can share
in the genuine chemistry that's passing between Donovan and Kara
at this special moment. See also other monologs from this play
included in the section of monologs for women.*

1   DONOVAN: You know, Kara, I've thought about this, and I've
2   decided it's completely wrong for me to take advantage of
3   the fact that you're not talking at the moment. So, of
4   course, I'm going to do it. I did try, in the last few weeks,
5   to talk to you, while you were talking, but you're always
6   involved. You know, you're probably the weirdest girl in
7   school — that's your nickname, Weird Kara, did you know
8   that? And the way you dress — I understand that you
9   *design* those clothes? And here you are all in black doing
10   something I really admire. Taking into consideration the
11   clothes you wore to last year's prom, the ones that made
12   you look like ... a ... colorful ... bowl of ... squashes ... I was

1 hoping you would go to the prom with me this year.
2 *(Pause.)* No, no, don't answer now. Please think about it. I
3 made this ... *(He removes a piece of paper from his pocket)* ...
4 flyer about what I expect on a prom date with you – lots of
5 eating, laughing, serious talk about your sister, a peek
6 under all that ... weirdness, and a prom dress that just
7 might be all black. It has my e-mail on it, in case you're too
8 busy to actually talk to me in the next two months. *(He
9 tucks it into her pocket.)* OK. Have a great evening. And
10 thank you all for coming out to do this. The world needs
11 more of you. Good for you, Weird Kara.

Additional Resources

Tip Sheet for
Preparing Presentations

Once you've settled upon the staging of your scene or monolog, review the following checklist for movements and stage positions. It will help you to sharpen the choices you've just made and avoid any basic pitfalls before you present your work to someone else.

1. Always face downstage when you introduce yourself and your recital selections, when you perform (as much as possible), and during the "thank you" after finishing. This will give spectators maximum opportunity to look at you and see you as a person; they're not interested in your back or your profile. In the case of a two-character scene, you should also introduce your scene partner (you should do all the talking).

2. Search for ways to "open" the scene or monolog to the audience whenever possible. When presenting a monolog, never play to empty chairs or imaginary doors or imaginary characters to the extreme sides of the space. Share your decisions, frustrations, choices, fears, doubts, etc. with the listeners. Also try this same approach in two-character scenes, whenever possible and appropriate.

3. When presenting a monolog, never deliver your piece to the directors, judges, or any other special person as the imaginary listener or audience. He or she has enough to do considering your acting skills without being made to feel obliged to give you a response.

4. Be certain that your acting partner in two-character scenes is also visible to the audience, although in a less emphatic position on-stage; and be sure to involve him or her in the scene. Create a relationship! In two-character scenes, the energy must be shared, and chemistry between you both must become palpable.

5. In a monolog, place your imaginary listener, the vis-à-vis, downstage from you, either to the left or right in the audience. Fix the location of that listener definitely in one place and always speak to him or her at that point. Never try to speak to an imaginary listener who has moved elsewhere on-stage, and never try to speak to one who is supposedly moving about, or you will appear to be losing focus.

6. You may have moments in a scene or monolog where the character (you!) is speaking off into space: dreamlike, nostalgic, recalling events, etc. Be certain at these moments that you speak out to the house, over the auditors' heads, and that your eye focus is always steadily on that point. Find only one definite place in the auditorium in order to anchor your visual focus at such moments.

7. Never pantomime actions such as drinking, smoking, knocking at a door, applying makeup, fighting, etc. Either discover a way to eliminate these actions, or, if worse comes to worst, bring a small hand prop with you for the purpose.

8. Play the monolog or scene as far downstage as possible, and use what furniture there is in the space, but beware of hiding behind it or having it block you.

9. Always rehearse with only one or two chairs, and if they give you more to work with at the actual audition — chairs, boxes, tables, or stools — by all means be ready to use it somehow.

10. Consider carefully whether or not you should actually sit in a chair. Most actors find that sitting will rob them of energy during the performance. Consider what other ways you might discover for using that chair or prop: to lean against, to move or adjust slightly, etc.

11. Rehearse your scene or monolog in very different spaces: small, large, a stage, an empty classroom, etc. Not only will this prepare you for whatever space you encounter at the actual presentation, but it will help add variety to keep you on your toes so your recital pieces stay fresh. It will also help to rehearse with your scene partner — he or she needs practice!

12. Rehearse your personal introduction as carefully as your recital piece, including your movement to and from the stage. The spectators are *always* watching you for clues! Never take more than a few seconds to begin your piece, and avoid fussing about with the furniture! Always remember that no matter how brief this personal introduction may be, it's a golden opportunity for you to speak as yourself — not as the character. So be warm, sincere, and confident.

13. Remember that in every performance, the other character you're presenting is you! So make a confident but relaxed entrance, and introduce yourself and your pieces pleasantly

and clearly. This is the real you, and the character is different. When you're finished, a simple "thank you" and a businesslike exit will suffice. Don't hang around and fidget. If they want to speak with you, they'll tell you straight out. And don't forget to smile!

14. Never stare at the stage floor! There is nothing there! Create a relationship with *someone*!

15. If you bobble a word or a phrase, never go back and start again, and never, ever apologize! Crash right on!

Studio and Individual Exercises for Performing Scenes and Monologs

General Exercises for Developing Presentation Skills

Exercise #1: Reading Aloud

For at least twenty minutes each day, go someplace where you can be alone without anyone hearing or distracting you, and read aloud. You can and should do this indoors and out. You can and should choose everything possible to read that you can lay your hands on: cookbooks, newspapers, textbooks, the stock reports, the telephone book, fairy tales, *War and Peace*, computer manuals, product assembly instructions, *Hamlet*, cereal boxes, the Bible, this anthology, etc. This should be material that you've never seen before. As you grow more skilled with this exercise, you can concentrate on different types of dramatic material (comedies, tragedies, melodramas, classical, contemporary, etc.). Practice holding the pages in one hand and reading aloud with expressiveness, energy, and animation. You need to pay special attention to several things while doing this exercise. First, you need to *learn to read smoothly, fluently, without hesitation.* Struggle to get your tongue around difficult and unfamiliar words, and look up jargon and technical language in a dictionary with pronunciation until you can master the text like a pro. Once you've gotten on top of that, try to *look up from the page as you read*, by training your eye to scan ahead a few words or phrases, and by moving your thumb down the page as you read in order to keep your place. Also learn to hold your script away from your face and somewhat to the side. These techniques will enable you to be clearly seen by the auditors, and to establish eye contact with your acting partner or imaginary listener. Third, you also need to move and gesture as you read *so you don't become a "talking head" on-stage. Do this exercise religiously every single day*, and I guarantee that your acting will show an immediate improvement, especially as you apply yourself to other reading-related courses in English, foreign language, literature, and the liberal arts.

Exercise #2: Verbal Resumé

Write a 250-word, one-paragraph prose statement of your performance experience. Highlight the best roles you've played, fun things you've done backstage, special classes and training you enjoyed, your career goals, some great shows you've been involved in, your major learning experiences, etc. Then practice delivering this "verbal resumé" out loud so you can speak it confidently, smoothly, and above all naturally — just like lines from a play! When you have your statement down to sixty seconds, try it out for your drama class and see what they think! Did you stress the right things about your background? Are there things you omitted that they think you should mention? Was it well-memorized so that you could look them in the eye as you spoke and communicate sincerity? Did you sound and look happy and upbeat about your self-description? And did it seem natural and unforced (not something memorized and recited for class)? You can keep practicing this verbal resumé at different times throughout your career, because more and more you'll find yourself relying on it when people ask you who you are and what you've done! By the way, if anyone important does ask you a question following your performance — that'll be what they ask. So don't get caught tongue-tied at that moment!

Exercise #3: Role-Playing and Role-Playing

Memorize the first ten to fifteen seconds of the opening of any monolog or scene and attempt to deliver the words as sincerely and expressively as possible, given what you believe to be the character's situation. For purposes of this exercise, reduce all your physical stage movements (blocking) to a minimum for those fifteen seconds, concentrating instead on the sincerity of the statement, your belief in the dramatic situation, and the character's mood while speaking. If possible, observe yourself in a full-length mirror while doing this in order to keep it physically simple and uncluttered. Once this has been well-memorized, rehearsed, and set — physically and vocally — prepare an introductory statement to add to it, as follows: "Hello! I'm Jane Brown. Today I'd like to present to you a selection from John Doe's play, *Here Is the Name of the Play*." Now connect your introductory statement to the monolog you've just rehearsed, *trying to represent your true personality as sincerely as possible, in contrast to the dramatic character you're about to enact.*

Practice this with a simple entrance where you come before the class or on-stage, introduce yourself and your piece to the group, and then turn your back to the group for one or two beats before beginning the character monolog. Did you succeed? Did the class see two different characters on-stage? Did the exercise make you feel that your real name and purpose actually sounded somewhat phony? Or did the character become phony? Maybe *neither* was phony? Did you truly feel you were giving the class the real you or the important you before the character monolog? Did the two blur? Were they both sincere? (Tip: both the characters are you. You *are* the role. An actor is a person specially gifted at playing roles.)

Exercises for Developing Vocal and Verbal Resources

Exercise #4: Adventures in Paraphrasing

Select any speech or scene from this text and write a denotative paraphrase of the speech (or one of the longer sections of the scene) that expresses the *literal or dictionary* definition of the text. Do not try to express the *emotional or underlying* meaning with your denotative paraphrase. In other words, put the speech into your own words, minus the "implications" or innuendoes between the lines and without adding anything. Now comment upon at least three ways in which the playwright's language differs from yours, and why that's important. Next, write a connotative paraphrase of the speech, one that captures the *emotional or underlying* message. This restatement of the text should be much longer, and should aim to express all the emotional intensity contained in the original — but in your own words. In two-character scenes with dialog, do the same thing: capture the energy and spirit of the emotional underpinnings of your character in the scene. It's important that you take some liberties with your paraphrase in order to capture the energy level, the emotional intensity of the original. In fact, you should ignore all grammar and syntax in your paraphrase in order to capture strong, raw emotion. Then find three reasons why the character's original words conceal the powerful emotional currents you found between the lines.

Exercise #5: Speaking the Denotative Paraphrase

The next step is to practice the speech or scene aloud, trying to *keep only the literal meanings clearly in mind as you speak*. Avoid the temptation to rush and to run together words and phrases, and don't pantomime anything except in the most difficult passages. Savor the images in your mind before they enter your mouth. Try to deliver the text with as much clarity of expression as possible and to motivate your delivery so it seems natural. When you feel you're ready, test yourself by having someone listen to you. Ask that person how much of the speech or scene was understandable the first time through (75% is a good average). Also ask how much of it seemed motivated and believable.

Exercise #6: Speaking the Connotative Paraphrase
Now deliver the monolog or scene and try to *keep only the connotative meanings in mind*. Afterwards, ask your listener how the literal sense of the speech or scene seemed to change. This is by far the most difficult part of the exercise. You might begin by whispering the subtext several times before gradually moving into a whispered delivery of the text. Gradually increase your volume until you can speak in a full stage voice without losing touch with the subtext. You can also practice this with a tape recorder. Record the connotative paraphrase with great intensity and allow it to play alongside you (or even better, with an earphone plug in your ear) underneath your delivery of the lines. Most importantly, give in to all your impulses for moving and gesturing, and for radical vocal delivery patterns that the subtext may suggest.

Exercise #7: Paraphrasing and Improvisation
This fun exercise is designed to help you fine-tune your paraphrases. Select any monolog or scene to work on. Read the original text aloud several times using an obviously false and unreal character voice from your favorite cartoon character. Donald Duck, Scooby-Doo, SpongeBob, and others can all be excellent choices. Let yourself go and have fun with this improv (two-character scenes can be especially hilarious). In fact, the more serious lines might even be the most fun of all when done with a ridiculous character voice! Each time you finish a reading, note in your journal what bizarre images, situations, double-meanings, or interpretations of the text the cartoon voice brought to mind. If you do this exercise correctly, you should find some different spots to note each time you read the material; and some of those connotations should also be retained in the finished paraphrase as valuable insights into what's happening in the text. You might also bring one or two of these cartoon readings into class and present it publicly to a group in order to get some feedback from others.

Exercise #8: Ripping Your Tongue Out

Pick any speech or scene and memorize it. Rehearse it as dramatically as possible for presentation to the class, including movements, vocal expressiveness, etc. Once you have it finally prepared, and are confident that you're performing all the ideas and emotions contained in the piece to the best of your ability, *try to perform it without words!* Try to communicate all the ideas and emotions through body language alone. You may certainly exaggerate your movements and act out your thoughts and feelings in any way you choose in this nonverbal performance (roll on the floor, stomp your feet, clap your hands, jump around, etc.); but you must not revert to any type of sign language like a charades game in order to get your point across. Then, once you've explored all the movement possibilities for communicating the sense and action of piece, you should try to speak the original words in gobbledygook language: nonsense sounds that capture the rhythm, inflections, and emphases of the original. Rehearse the piece exploring combinations of both nonverbal movements as well as gobbledygook in order to communicate the original material as effectively as you can. With two-character scenes, this exercise should be done with only one character either pantomiming or speaking in gobbledygook. Then bring it to class and see from the responses you receive how well you've succeeded!

Exercise #9: Exploring Vowel Sounds

In the very best writers you'll find more than simply a *literary* command of words in the form of vocabulary, sentence structure, narration, and such things; you'll also find a strong and vital command of the *sound* of words as they ring in the listeners' ears. This is, of course, particularly true of great poets and playwrights, and you should always read poetry and plays aloud in order to fully appreciate them. In this exercise you should speak the lines of your monolog or scene very, very slowly, noting your identification of operative words and phrases as you talk, and stretching or unnaturally elongating all the vowel sounds. It will sound very odd to you, but don't be put off; stay with it! Roll the sounds around in your mouth; let them resonate and trill as you deliver the words until you feel like you're almost making opera music! This should sensitize you to any hidden *vocal* qualities of the language that the playwright has embedded in the writing.

Then gradually bring your delivery up to speed, stressing a little more those words and phrases where you just discovered the vowel sounds to have special importance in adding emphasis to the ideas. This exercise can then move to an advanced level where you concentrate upon the sound patterns of phrases and complete sentences, rather than only upon the sound of individual words. Here you'll discover the other poetic qualities of the text such as rhythm and meter.

Exercise #10: Exploring Consonant Sounds

Just as with vowel or tonal sounds, you'll find a strong and vital command of the *consonant sounds* in words as they ring in the listeners' ears. Speak the lines of your monolog or scene very, very slowly, over-exaggerating the consonant sounds in the text. Again, it will sound very odd to you, but don't be put off; stay with it! Chew-out the consonants, pound them where it seems appropriate, glide or hiss them, and sensitize yourself to any hidden vocal qualities of the language that the playwright has embedded in the writing. Then gradually bring your delivery up to speed, trying to speak the text more naturally and stressing a little more those words and phrases where you just discovered the consonant sounds to have special importance in adding emphasis. By stressing the consonants in this way you'll find not only that you can greatly enhance the meaning of the text, but also that your stage speech is becoming more clear and that it projects better, without raising the volume of your voice! Why? Because it is the actor's pronunciation of the *consonants* that accounts more than anything else for the quality of his or her projection in live performance!

Exercises for Playing Dramatic Structure
Exercise #11: Eventing the Script

This exercise is valuable for identifying and playing the high points of your material and strengthening the overall development of scenes or monologs. After first reading your monolog or scene, write down a list of all the important ideas you feel the material is conveying. Now reduce that list to no more than two or three ideas. This is hard! Now identify in which sections of your script these ideas are most clearly stated. Those are the places where the events change, and we call these larger sections of the speech or scene the "beats" or "bits." At those points in the scene or monolog, your audience *must see* things happening to you. These are the points where *you must make something happen to you in the scene!* Do you discover/decide upon/reject/accept an idea or an action at that point? Whatever you decide, play that decision or discovery fully and expressively, making us see a sharp contrast with the decision or discovery that just preceded it. In order to identify these sections, draw a line across the page at points where the beats change. More than one pattern of events is possible, so feel free to change these two to three beats as you explore your recital piece in this way until you're satisfied and comfortable making an event out of each of those two to three building blocks that you've identified. Now you must keep reading your piece aloud over and over, eventing the narrative in this way, until you discover how these events add up — how they get you somewhere different at the end of the monolog or scene than where you began. We must see this development happening to you. You *must* become someone different, something *must* change and happen to you as a result of the scene or monolog, or you're not presenting the piece correctly.

Many beginning actors make the mistake of trying to emphasize *every* idea in the speech or scene, or trying to find *too much* to emphasize. But you can only play one action at a time, and the number of ideas must be kept small in order for them to be clearly perceived and effective.

Exercise #12: Peaks and Valleys

This exercise builds upon the previous one and is valuable for developing variety in your presentation. After eventing your script, you must now identify the *rhythm* of the scene or monolog. This means controlling the *pace* of the action and the *emotional intensity or urgency in pursuing your goals* as the scene develops. For example, do you think the excitement in the scene builds steadily and relentlessly towards a climax? That the events your character experiences build steadily in their intensity? Then the intensity and pace of your vocal energy and physical excitement should also build the same way. Do you feel, however, that the action in the speech or scene develops more like stepping stones, moving from one climax to the next? Then how quickly and with what intensity do those climactic points follow one another? What's their pattern? In either case, your interpretation should display vocal and physical variety that corresponds to the sense of what you're speaking, and we should notice that. Things happen in the speech or scene; things change. Emotional variety, variations in vocal pitch and volume, the speed and quality of your movements — all of these reflect such changes, reflect the sense of the words, and this is what we should see. If you omit this step in your rehearsals, then your presentation is likely to seem like a one-note samba, monotonous and mechanical.

Some actors find it helpful to outline this structure in their text by means of a "fever chart," writing numbers beside the beats in the margin to indicate levels of intensity. Using a simple scale from one through ten, you can easily remind yourself in this way of the shifting pattern of builds and climaxes that you've discovered in your material, and make your presentation more dynamic. This exercise is very important for young actors who tend to play scenes and monologs entirely at the same level. Beginning actors, for example, will plead and suffer through the entire piece, or will play anger or seduction from beginning to end. This is extremely boring, though, for a spectator. Instead, you should train yourself to identify a wide range of emotional colors on your palette; and if you look closely at the speech or the scene, you will find them!

Exercises for Developing Physical Resources
Exercise #13: Physical Objects Improvisation
Fill your rehearsal space with as many different large objects and pieces of furniture as you can locate: chairs, stools, tables, a broom, bottles, a bicycle, several large cardboard boxes, books, a sofa, a telephone, a laundry basket, etc. As you speak the monolog or act the scene with your partner, try to make physical contact with *everything* in the room at least once, including the walls and the floor. This doesn't mean that you necessarily have to use these objects extensively, such as sitting in a chair or riding the bicycle or folding the laundry; simply touching or relocating them will often suffice. The point of this exercise is to concretize the ideas in your own mind, to ground the text in some sense of physical, spatial reality. In actual performance, of course, you will normally have no props or furniture to use, but you should find that introducing physical exercises to your movement improvisations will stimulate even more ideas for staging the piece later.

Exercise #14: Life Gesture

Before beginning any movement, spend a few minutes thinking about the dramatic character and his or her physical appearance. Ask yourself if there is some distinguishing movement, posture, muscle tone, or physical mannerism that is unique to him or her — a life gesture that seems to characterize that person. We all have such life gestures: hooking our hands on our belts, flicking hair from our face, standing with arms akimbo, scratching ourselves, folding our arms, etc. Try to discover a gesture that's appropriate for the dramatic character based upon everything you know about the entire play. The gesture may or may not be performed; you should make the choice whether or not it becomes actually overt. Experiment with several possibilities using different lines from the monolog or scene until you hit upon one that seems right to you — one that seems to encapsulate the character's attitude best. The final step is to try to perform the scene or monolog using the gesture here and there, to gain a sense of characterizing by physicalizing the role. If you're successful, this physicalization will be different from your own behavior! Until you gain a concrete sense of how physically different the dramatic character is from your real self, then you haven't gone far enough in your characterization

Exploring Computer Resources for Acting Careers
Exercise 15: Actors on the Internet

Take an hour to visit either of these fun Web sites for actors: "The Thespian Net" at http://thespiannet.com/, or "AWOL" (Acting Workshop On-Line) and its links at http://redbirdstudio.com/AWOL/acting2.html. Investigate how the actors you find there are using computer networking to stay in touch with one another. Be sure to explore some of the links at each site! Do the actors have specific questions they want answered? An audience to listen to their problems or share their successes? Are they seeking friends in industry locations, or inside information on various acting markets? Where are they networking from, where are they living, and does that really matter? Does it seem they're new actors just getting started, or actors who are already established to some degree? Click on the links there to other actors' Web sites both in the U.S. and overseas to see the range of possibilities that are currently being exploited on the World Wide Web. Does it look like some actors are actually finding work this way through the Internet? Why are they exerting such effort to jump into cyberspace in this way? What exactly is their payoff? Now locate at least two other actors' Web sites that you've discovered, and then write a two to three page report on everything you've found on the World Wide Web in this exercise, including important new links you've uncovered on your own, and present it to the class.

Exercise 16: Scope Out the Union #1

Do you want to learn what it means to be a union actor? See what professional acting unions offer actors? What you might face one day after you're out of school? Visit www.sag.org, the Web site of the Screen Actors' Guild. Click the "FAQ" link at the top of the home page, then click "Getting Started as an Actor" on the left sidebar. What advice do they give you about breaking into the movies? Click on the link at the top of the page entitled "Join SAG." What are the eligibility requirements to join the screen actors union? Go back to the home page and click on the link "News and Events," read any two of the current reports or press releases there, and choose one for an oral report to your class.

Exercise #17: Scope Out the Union #2

Curious about professional-level stage acting in the United States and what you might have to know once you leave school and enter "the biz?" Go to the Actors Equity Association Web site: www.actorsequity.org. Read through this Web site in order to get an overview of all the main issues affecting people today in the profession you might someday want to enter. Read through those sections called "About Equity," "Membership Responsibilities," and the "Casting Call." After you've read awhile, write up a report on what is expected of a union actor, what the union can do for an actor, what's the procedure for joining the union, or what does a union actor earn? Present your report to your drama class.

Exploration #18: Cyberphotos

Wondering about publicity headshots and how to start building your cyber-resume? Visit the following Web site: www.takeoneacting.com. How would you describe the purpose, range, and usefulness of this Web site? Click on the link entitled "Headshot Info." What do you find there about photographs that's surprisingly new to you? Click on "Resume Info" and then go to www.actingresume.com. What does this service provide? Be sure to click on "Get Your Act Together" and explore this link thoroughly. There you'll find a section on terminology where you can test yourself — are there terms you should know about? You'll also find a section on wardrobe. Have you ever given serious thought to a dress code for actors? Write up a report and present it to your drama class!

Exercise #19: Audition Tips and Requirements
Divide your class into three teams, each of which investigates one of the following Web sites: The Kennedy Center American College Theatre Festival (www.kennedy-center.org/education/actf/), the University/Resident Theatre Association (www.urta.com), and the Actors Equity Association (www.actorsequity.org). Each team member should list what he or she regards as the most important audition advice given by each organization as well as important background information about each organization that a serious actor should know about. The team then prepares a ten-minute report for the entire class that explains the following:

- What is the nature of the organization? Its stated mission? Its history? Its perceived importance? Who participates in its activities, and what is the range of these activities? What services does it offer actors?
- What does this organization recommend as far as auditioning is concerned? What are the requirements (if any)? What sort of tips does it provide? Does it refer actors to any additional sources for further information? If so, what are they?
- What sort of costs are incurred by individuals wishing to participate in the activities of this organization? What are the benefits (as far as you can determine)?

Really Useful Books for Building Auditioning and Forensics Skills

Monolog and Scene Anthologies Since 2000

There are a huge number of monolog and scene anthologies on the market today, both for legitimate theatre as well as for the media. As a result, it's often difficult to choose those appropriate for a specific purpose: auditioning pieces, forensics exercises, TV auditions, acting class assignments, camera projects, religious-gender-multicultural topics, and so forth. The following list confines itself only to those dealing with stage acting, and I recommend these for young actors for several reasons:

- These books have been published within the last five years, so they obviously contain the most current material in terms of content, relevance to the concerns of young actors, and originality in the writing;
- These books are specifically designed for young actors. Anthologies that lack some indication in their title as "suitable for certain age groups" will surely contain a lot of scenes and monologs for older, more mature characters whose emotional range is likely to be outside that of younger actors. I have, however, included a few of these "older characters" collections here simply because of their popularity with my students at the university level.
- Most of the books in this list also contain acting prefaces and tips that are often helpful for self-rehearsal.

Alterman, Glen. *The Perfect Audition Monologue*. Manchester, NH: Smith and Kraus, 2003.

———. *Two Minutes and More: Even More Original Character Monologues*. Manchester, NH: Smith and Kraus, 2004.

Beard, Jocelyn. *The Best Women's Stage Monologues of 2000*. Manchester, NH: Smith and Kraus, 2001. (Subsequent editions through 2004.)

———. *The Best Men's Stage Monologues of 2000*. Manchester, NH: Smith and Kraus, 2002. (Subsequent editions through 2004.)

Coen, Stephanie. *American Theatre Book of Monologues for Women*. New York: Theatre Communications Group, 2001.

———. *American Theatre Book of Monologues for Men*. New York: Theatre Communications Group, 2001.

Craig, David. *On Singing Onstage*. New York: Applause, 2000.

Dunmore, Simon, ed. *More Alternative Shakespeare Auditions for Women*. New York: Routledge, 2000, and Volume 2, 2002.

Earley, Michael and Philippa Keil. *Soliloquy: The Shakespeare Monologues for Women*. New York: Applause, 2000.

——. *Solo! The Best Monologues of the 80s*. New York: Applause, 2000.

Ellis, Roger. *Audition Monologs for Student Actors 2: Selections from Contemporary Plays*. Colorado Springs: Meriwether, 2001.

——. *New Audition Scenes and Monologs from Contemporary Playwrights*. Colorado Springs: Meriwether, 2005.

Gale, Steven. *Outstanding Stage Monologs and Scenes from the '90s*. Colorado Springs: Meriwether, 2000.

Henderson, Heather H. *The Flip Side II: 64 More Point-of-View Monologs for Teens*. Colorado Springs: Meriwether, 2001.

James, Steven. *On the Edge: A Collection of 17 Hard-Hitting Christian Monologs for Youth*. Colorado Springs: Meriwether, 2004.

Katz, Leon. *Classical Monologues for Women*. New York: Applause, 2004.

——. *Classical Monologues for Younger Men*. New York: Applause, 2002.

Kluger, Garry Michael. *Fifty More Professional Scenes and Monologs for Student Actors*. Colorado Springs: Meriwether, 2004.

Lepidus, D.L. *The Best Women's Stage Monologues of 2001*. (Subsequent volumes through 2004.) Manchester, NH: Smith and Kraus, 2001-2004.

——. *The Best Men's Stage Monologues of 2001*. (Subsequent volumes through 2004.) Manchester, NH: Smith and Kraus, 2001-2004.

——. *The Best Stage Scenes of 2001*. (Subsequent volumes through 2004.) Manchester, NH: Smith and Kraus, 2001-2004.

Lightfoot, D. Tulla. *The Spirit of America: Patriotic Monologues and Speeches for Middle and High School Students*. Manchester, NH: Smith and Kraus, 2005.

Maddox, Deborah. *Audition Monologues: Power Pieces for Women*. Mesa, AZ: Lucid Solutions, 2003.

——. *Audition Monologues: Power Pieces for Kids and Teens*. Mesa, AZ: Lucid Solutions, 2002.

Marlow, Jean. *Audition Speeches for Men.* New York: Theatre Arts, 2001.

——. *Audition Speeches for Women.* New York: Theatre Arts, 2001.

——. *Audition Speeches for Younger Actors 16+.* New York: Theatre Arts, 2002.

——. *Audition Speeches for 6-16 Year Olds.* New York: Theatre Arts, 2002.

McCormick, Kimberley A. *The Way I See It: 50 Values-Oriented Monologs for Teens.* Colorado Springs: Meriwether, 2001.

McKenna, Shaun, ed. *Contemporary Scenes for Young Women.* New York: Theatre Communications Group, 2000.

Milstein, Janet B. and L.E. McCullough. *The Ultimate Audition Book for Teens: 111 One-Minute Monologues.* Manchester, NH: Smith and Kraus, 2000, and Volume 2, 2005.

——. *Cool Characters for Kids: 71 One-Minute Monologues.* Manchester, NH: Smith and Kraus, 2004.

Ratliff, Gerald Lee. *Millenium Monologs: 95 Contemporary Characterizations for Young Actors.* Colorado Springs: Meriwether, 2002.

——. *Young Women's Monologs from Contemporary Plays.* Colorado Springs: Meriwether, 2004.

Sanders, Francesca. *Look Deeper: A Collections of Monologs for Young Women — A Multicultural Collection.* Odessa, TX: Brooklyn, 2002.

Sullivan, T.G. *Short Contest Monologs for Teen Women.* Odessa, TX: Brooklyn, 2002.

Ullom, Shirley. *Tough Acts to Follow: Seventy-five Monologs for Teens.* Colorado Springs: Meriwether, 2000.

Young, Rebecca. *100 Great Monologs.* Colorado Springs: Meriwether, 2005.

——. *Famous Fantasy Character Monologs.* Colorado Springs: Meriwether, 2006.

Popular How-To-Audition Texts (1980 – 2000)

None of the following books are specifically geared to young actors. Practically all are written for professionals, and younger actors may be unfamiliar with many of the plays and references the authors make in their texts. However, all contain useful suggestions for improving one's general acting abilities, as well as for making more effective choices in auditions. Though some of these texts are a bit dated, they all contain excellent advice and effective methods for training actors in the various skill areas. And all of these deal strictly with live theatre.

Black, David. *The Actor's Audition*. New York: Vintage, 1997.

Hunt, Gordon. *How to Audition*. New York: Harper Collins, 1995.

Oliver, Donald. *How to Audition for the Musical Theatre*. Manchester, NH: Smith and Kraus, 1995.

Ratliff, Gerald Lee. *The Theatre Audition Book: Playing Monologs from Contemporary, Modern, Period, Shakespeare, and Classical Plays*. Colorado Springs: Meriwether, 1998.

Shurtleff, Michael. *Audition: Everything an Actor Needs to Know to Get the Part*. New York: Walker, 1984.

Silver, Fred. *Auditioning for the Musical Theatre*. New York: Penguin, 1988.

Popular How-To-Audition Texts (2000 – 2005)

These are the most popular recent additions to the field. Only one of them (my own) is set up as a class or studio textbook with step-by-step methods for skill development, solo or group exercises, etc. All of them contain broad application of performance skills to other fields like accessing Internet-based acting resources, job-hunting, forensics competitions, film and television presentations, etc. They all focus upon legitimate theatre auditions.

Ellis, Roger. *The Complete Audition Book for Young Actors*. Colorado Springs: Meriwether, 2003.

Flinn, Denny Martin and Ellie Kanner. *How Not to Audition: Avoiding Common Mistakes Most Actors Make*. Hollywood: Lone Eagle, 2003.

Kayes, Gillyanne and Jeremy Fisher. *Successful Singing Auditions*. New York: Theatre Arts, 2002.

Merlin, Joanna. *Auditioning*. New York: Vintage, 2001.

Credits

120 Lives a Minute by Gustavo Ott, tr. Heather L. McKay. © 2006 by Gustavo Ott, tr. Heather L. McKay. Reprinted by permission. Professionals and amateurs are hereby warned that performances of *120 Lives a Minute* are subject to a royalty. It is fully protected under the copyright laws of the United States of America, and of all countries covered by the International Copyright union (including the Dominion of Canada and the rest of the British Commonwealth), and of all countries covered by the Pan-American Copyright Convention and the Universal Copyright Convention, and of all countries with which the United States has reciprocal copyright relations. All rights, including professional, amateur, motion picture, recitation, lecturing, public reading, radio broadcasting, television, video or sound taping, all other forms of mechanical or electronic reproductions, such as information storage and retrieval systems and photocopying, and the rights of translation into foreign languages, are strictly reserved. Particular emphasis is laid upon the question of readings, permission for which must be secured from the author in writing. Information concerning rights should be addressed to the author: Gustavo Ott, 5093 White Pine Circle NE, St. Petersburg, FL 33703-3139. E-mail: gustavott@yahoo.com. Web site: www.gustavoott.com.ar.

Addiction by Joel Murray. © 2004 by Joel Murray, all rights reserved. Professionals and amateurs are hereby warned that performances of *Addiction* are subject to a royalty. It is fully protected under the copyright laws of the United States of America, and of all countries covered by the International Copyright union (including the Dominion of Canada and the rest of the British Commonwealth), and of all countries covered by the Pan-American Copyright Convention and the Universal Copyright Convention, and of all countries with which the United States has reciprocal copyright relations. All rights, including professional, amateur, motion picture, recitation, lecturing, public reading, radio broadcasting, television, video or sound taping, all other forms of mechanical or electronic reproductions, such as information storage and retrieval systems and photocopying, and the rights of translation into foreign languages, are strictly reserved. Particular emphasis is laid upon the question of readings, permission for which must be secured from the author in writing. Contact Joel Murray at jmurray@utep.edu.

American Midget by Jonathan Yukich. © 2004 by Jonathan Yukich, all rights reserved. Professionals and amateurs are hereby warned that performances of *American Midget* are subject to a royalty. It is fully protected under the copyright laws of the United States of America, and of all countries covered by the International Copyright union (including the Dominion of Canada and the rest of the British Commonwealth), and of all countries covered by the Pan-American Copyright Convention and the Universal Copyright Convention, and of all countries with which the United States has reciprocal copyright relations. All rights, including professional, amateur, motion picture, recitation, lecturing, public reading, radio broadcasting, television, video or sound taping, all other forms of mechanical or electronic reproductions, such as information storage and retrieval systems and photocopying, and the rights of translation into foreign languages, are strictly reserved. Particular emphasis is laid upon the question of readings, permission for which must be secured from the author in writing. Contact Jonathan Yukich at yukich5@yahoo.com.

BFE by Julia Cho, © 2005 by Julia Cho. Professionals and amateurs are hereby warned that performances of *BFE* are subject to a royalty. It is fully protected under the copyright laws of the United States of America, and of all countries covered by the International Copyright union (including the Dominion of Canada and the rest of the British Commonwealth), and of all countries covered by the Pan-American Copyright Convention and the Universal Copyright Convention, and of all countries with which the United States has reciprocal copyright relations. All rights, including professional, amateur, motion picture, recitation, lecturing, public reading, radio broadcasting, television, video or sound taping, all other forms of mechanical or electronic reproductions, such as information storage and retrieval systems and photocopying, and the rights of translation into foreign languages, are strictly reserved. Particular emphasis is laid upon the question of readings, permission for which must be secured from the author's agent in writing. All inquiries regarding rights should be addressed to John Buzzetti, The Gersh Agency, 41 Madison Ave., 33rd floor, New York, NY 10010, (212) 997-1818.

Big Girl by Andrew Biss. © 2005 by Andrew Biss, all rights reserved. Professionals and amateurs are hereby warned that performances of *Big Girl* are subject to a royalty. It is fully protected under the copyright laws of the United States of America, and of all countries covered by the International Copyright union (including the Dominion of Canada and the rest of the British Commonwealth), and of all countries covered by the Pan-American Copyright Convention and the Universal Copyright Convention, and of all countries with which the United States has reciprocal copyright relations. All rights, including professional, amateur, motion picture, recitation, lecturing, public reading, radio broadcasting, television, video or sound taping, all other forms of mechanical or electronic reproductions, such as information storage and retrieval systems and photocopying, and the rights of translation into foreign languages, are strictly reserved. Particular emphasis is laid upon the question of readings, permission for which must be secured from the author in writing. Contact Andrew Biss at andrewbiss@hotmail.com.

By Looking from *The Pink Plays* by Kerri Kochanski. © 2004 by Kerri Kochanski, all rights reserved. Professionals and amateurs are hereby warned that performances of *By Looking* are subject to a royalty. It is fully protected under the copyright laws of the United States of America, and of all countries covered by the International Copyright union (including the Dominion of Canada and the rest of the British Commonwealth), and of all countries covered by the Pan-American Copyright Convention and the Universal Copyright Convention, and of all countries with which the United States has reciprocal copyright relations. All rights, including professional, amateur, motion picture, recitation, lecturing, public reading, radio broadcasting, television, video or sound taping, all other forms of mechanical or electronic reproductions, such as information storage and retrieval systems and photocopying, and the rights of translation into foreign languages, are strictly reserved. Particular emphasis is laid upon the question of readings, permission for which must be secured from the author in writing. Contact Kerri Kochanski at kerrikochanski@optonline.net.

Cell Cycle by Cristina Pippa. © 2005 by Cristina Pippa, all rights reserved. Professionals and amateurs are hereby warned that performances of *Cell Cycle* are subject to a royalty. It is fully protected under the copyright laws of the United States of America, and of all countries covered by the International Copyright union (including the Dominion of Canada and the rest of the British Commonwealth), and of all countries covered by the Pan-American Copyright Convention and the Universal Copyright Convention, and of all countries with which the United States has reciprocal copyright relations. All rights, including professional, amateur, motion picture, recitation, lecturing, public reading, radio broadcasting, television, video or sound taping, all other forms of mechanical or electronic reproductions, such as information storage and retrieval systems and photocopying, and the rights of translation into foreign languages, are strictly reserved. Particular emphasis is laid upon the question of readings, permission for which must be secured from the author in writing. Contact Cristina Pippa at cristinapippa@gmail.com.

The Children's Teeth by Nicolette Bethel. © 2003, 2005 by Nicolette Bethel, all rights reserved. Professionals and amateurs are hereby warned that performances of *The Children's Teeth* are subject to a royalty. It is fully protected under the copyright laws of the United States of America, and of all countries covered by the International Copyright union (including the Dominion of Canada and the rest of the British Commonwealth), and of all countries covered by the Pan-American Copyright Convention, and the Universal Copyright Convention, and of all countries with which the United States has

Deck the Stage by Lindsay Price. © 2005 by Lindsay Price, all rights reserved. Professionals and amateurs are hereby warned that performances of *Deck the Stage* are subject to a royalty. It is fully protected under the copyright laws of the United States of America, and of all countries covered by the International Copyright union (including the Dominion of Canada and the rest of the British Commonwealth), and of all countries covered by the Pan-American Copyright Convention and the Universal Copyright Convention, and of all countries with which the United States has reciprocal copyright relations. All rights, including professional, amateur, motion picture, recitation, lecturing, public reading, radio broadcasting, television, video or sound taping, all other forms of mechanical or electronic reproductions, such as information storage and retrieval systems and photocopying, and the rights of translation into foreign languages, are strictly reserved. Particular emphasis is laid upon the question of readings, permission for which must be secured from the author in writing. Contact Lindsay Price at Lindsay@theatrefolk.com.

A Different Place by Robin Graham. © 2001 by Robin Graham, all rights reserved. Professionals and amateurs are hereby warned that performances of *A Different Place* are subject to a royalty. It is fully protected under the copyright laws of the United States of America, and of all countries covered by the International Copyright union (including the Dominion of Canada and the rest of the British Commonwealth), and of all countries covered by the Pan-American Copyright Convention and the Universal Copyright Convention, and of all countries with which the United States has reciprocal copyright relations. All rights, including professional, amateur, motion picture, recitation, lecturing, public reading, radio broadcasting, television, video or sound taping, all other forms of mechanical or electronic reproductions, such as information storage and retrieval systems and photocopying, and the rights of translation into foreign languages, are strictly reserved. Particular emphasis is laid upon the question of readings, permission for which must be secured from the author in writing. Contact Robin Graham at robin@writelaugh.co.uk. Or visit her website: www.writelaugh.co.uk.

The Doe by Elise Geither. © 2005 by Elise Geither, all rights reserved. Professionals and amateurs are hereby warned that performances of *The Doe* are subject to a royalty. It is fully protected under the copyright laws of the United States of America, and of all countries covered by the International Copyright union (including the Dominion of Canada and the rest of the British Commonwealth), and of all countries covered by the Pan-American Copyright Convention and the Universal Copyright Convention, and of all countries with which the United States has reciprocal copyright relations. All rights, including professional, amateur, motion picture, recitation, lecturing, public reading, radio broadcasting, television, video or

relations. All rights, including professional, amateur, motion picture, recitation, lecturing, public reading, radio broadcasting, television, video or sound taping, all other forms of mechanical or electronic reproductions, such as information storage and retrieval systems and photocopying, and the rights of translation into foreign languages, are strictly reserved. Particular emphasis is laid upon the question of readings, permission for which must be secured from the author's agent in writing. All inquiries regarding rights should be addressed to: Mark H. Glick, Glick and Weintraub, 1501 Broadway, Suite 2401, New York, NY 10036-5601.

Harvest by Diane Lefer. © 2005 by Diane Lefer, all rights reserved. Professionals and amateurs are hereby warned that performances of *Harvest* are subject to a royalty. It is fully protected under the copyright laws of the United States of America, and of all countries covered by the International Copyright union (including the Dominion of Canada and the rest of the British Commonwealth), and of all countries covered by the Pan-American Copyright Convention and the Universal Copyright Convention, and of all countries with which the United States has reciprocal copyright relations. All rights, including professional, amateur, motion picture, recitation, lecturing, public reading, radio broadcasting, television, video or sound taping, all other forms of mechanical or electronic reproductions, such as information storage and retrieval systems and photocopying, and the rights of translation into foreign languages, are strictly reserved. Particular emphasis is laid upon the question of readings, permission for which must be secured from the author in writing. Contact Diane Lefer at DESILEF@cs.com.

Have Mercy by Hope McIntyre. © 2004 by Hope McIntyre, all rights reserved. Professionals and amateurs are hereby warned that performances of *Have Mercy* are subject to a royalty. It is fully protected under the copyright laws of the United States of America, and of all countries covered by the International Copyright union (including the Dominion of Canada and the rest of the British Commonwealth), and of all countries covered by the Pan-American Copyright Convention and the Universal Copyright Convention, and of all countries with which the United States has reciprocal copyright relations. All rights, including professional, amateur, motion picture, recitation, lecturing, public reading, radio broadcasting, television, video or sound taping, all other forms of mechanical or electronic reproductions, such as information storage and retrieval systems and photocopying, and the rights of translation into foreign languages, are strictly reserved. Particular emphasis is laid upon the question of readings, permission for which must be secured from the author in writing. Contact Hope McIntyre at raregem2@hotmail.com.

photocopying, and the rights of translation into foreign languages, are strictly reserved. Particular emphasis is laid upon the question of readings, permission for which must be secured from the author in writing. Contact Jonathan Wallace at jw@bway.net.

Shot At by Adam J. Ruben. © 2004 by Adam J. Ruben, all rights reserved. Professionals and amateurs are hereby warned that performances of *Shot At* are subject to a royalty. It is fully protected under the copyright laws of the United States of America, and of all countries covered by the International Copyright union (including the Dominion of Canada and the rest of the British Commonwealth), and of all countries covered by the Pan-American Copyright Convention and the Universal Copyright Convention, and of all countries with which the United States has reciprocal copyright relations. All rights, including professional, amateur, motion picture, recitation, lecturing, public reading, radio broadcasting, television, video or sound taping, all other forms of mechanical or electronic reproductions, such as information storage and retrieval systems and photocopying, and the rights of translation into foreign languages, are strictly reserved. Particular emphasis is laid upon the question of readings, permission for which must be secured from the author in writing. Contact Adam J. Ruben at ajruben@jhu.edu.

Skid Marks II by Lindsay Price. © 2005 by Lindsay Price, all rights reserved. Professionals and amateurs are hereby warned that performances of *Skid Marks II* are subject to a royalty. It is fully protected under the copyright laws of the United States of America, and of all countries covered by the International Copyright union (including the Dominion of Canada and the rest of the British Commonwealth), and of all countries covered by the Pan-American Copyright Convention and the Universal Copyright Convention, and of all countries with which the United States has reciprocal copyright relations. All rights, including professional, amateur, motion picture, recitation, lecturing, public reading, radio broadcasting, television, video or sound taping, all other forms of mechanical or electronic reproductions, such as information storage and retrieval systems and photocopying, and the rights of translation into foreign languages, are strictly reserved. Particular emphasis is laid upon the question of readings, permission for which must be secured from the author in writing. Contact Lindsay Price at Lindsay@theatrefolk.com.

The Story of the Panda Bears Told by a Saxophonist Who Has a Girlfriend in Frankfurt by Matéi Visniec, translated from the French by Claire Doucet and Ian Whitfield. © 1996 by Matéi Visniec, all rights reserved. Professionals and amateurs are hereby warned that performances of *The Story of the Panda Bears Told by a Saxophonist Who Has a Girlfriend in Frankfurt* are subject to a royalty. It is fully protected under the copyright laws of the United States of America,

About the Editor

Roger Ellis is a director, actor, and acting coach who has worked in professional, community, and university theatres in the United States and abroad for the past thirty years. An actor/director for seventeen years with Shakespeare Festivals in California and the Midwest, Dr. Ellis also coordinates the work of drama students with national and international theatre festivals, adjudicates high school and university performances, and conducts acting workshops; he has also edited and authored fourteen books on the contemporary theatre for North American publishers. A graduate of Cal Berkeley's doctoral program, he has trained and studied acting at Dell'Arte International and the American Conservatory Theatres in California, the Herbert Berghof Studios in New York, and with artists such as James Roose-Evans of the National Theatre of Great Britain, Michael Shurtleff, and Carlo Mazzone-Clementi. He is a professor of theatre communications at Grand Valley State University in Michigan, and the President of the Michigan Theatre Alliance where he now coordinates the efforts of theatre amateurs and professionals across the state.

Order Form

Meriwether Publishing Ltd.
PO Box 7710
Colorado Springs, CO 80933-7710
Phone: 800-937-5297 Fax: 719-594-9916
Website: www.meriwether.com

Please send me the following books:

_____ **More Scenes and Monologs from** $15.95
the Best New Plays #BK-B291
edited by Roger Ellis
An anthology of new dramatic writing from professionally produced plays

_____ **New Audition Scenes and Monologs** $15.95
from Contemporary Playwrights #BK-B278
edited by Roger Ellis
The best new cuttings from around the world

_____ **Audition Monologs for Student Actors** $15.95
#BK-B232

HVINW 808
.8245
M836   s II $15.95

Friends of the
Houston Public Library

_____ $19.95

MORE SCENES AND
MONOLOGS   *ing skills*

_____ VINSON $15.95
01/09

_____ **Young Women's Monologs from** $15.95
Contemporary Plays #BK-B272
edited by Gerald Lee Ratliff
Professional auditions for aspiring actresses

**These and other fine Meriwether Publishing books are available at
your local bookstore or direct from the publisher. Prices subject to
change without notice. Check our website or call for current prices.**

Name: _____ e-mail: _____

Organization name: _____

Address: _____

City: _____ State: _____

Zip: _____ Phone: _____

❑ **Check enclosed**

❑ **Visa / MasterCard / Discover #** _____

Signature: _____   Expiration
date: _____ / _____
(required for credit card orders)

Colorado residents: Please add 3% sales tax.
Shipping: Include $3.95 for the first book and 75¢ for each additional book ordered.

❑ *Please send me a copy of your complete catalog of books and plays.*